Sticky Knowledge

Barriers to Knowing in the Firm

Gabriel Szulanski

SAGE Publications
London • Thousand Oaks • New Delhi

SAGE Publications Ltd
6 Bonhill Street
London EC2A 4PU

SAGE Publications Inc.
2455 Teller Road
Thousand Oaks, California 91320

SAGE Publications India Pvt Ltd
B-42, Panchsheel Enclave
Post Box 4109
New Delhi 110 017

British Library Cataloguing in Publication data

A catalogue record for this book is available from
the British Library

ISBN 0 7619 6142 9
ISBN 0 7619 6143 7 (pbk)

Library of Congress Control Number available

Typeset by C&M Digitals (P) Ltd., Chennai, India
Printed and bound in Great Britain by Athenaeum Press, Galeshead

Sticky Knowledge

Sage Strategy Series

The objective of the *SAGE STRATEGY SERIES* is to publish significant contributions in the field of management in general, and strategy in particular. The books aim to make a scholarly and provocative contribution to the field of strategy, and are of a high intellectual standard, containing new contributions to the literature. We are especially interested in books which provide new insights into existing ideas, as well as those which challenge conventional thinking by linking together levels of analysis which were traditionally distinct.

A special feature of the series is that there is an active advisory board of strategy scholars from leading, international business schools in Europe, USA and the Far East who endorse the series. We believe that the combination of the Sage brand name and that of an active and strong board is a unique selling point for book buyers and other academics. The board is led by Professor Charles Baden-Fuller of City University Business School and the Rotterdam School of Management, and Richard Whittington of the Said Business School, University of Oxford.

Editors

Professor Charles Baden-Fuller, *City University Business School, London and Erasmus University, NL*
Professor Richard Whittington, *Said Business School, University of Oxford*

Editorial Board

Professor Frans van den Bosch, *Rotterdam School of Management, Erasmus University, NL*
✝ Professor Roland Calori, *EM Lyon, France*
Professor Robert Grant, *Georgetown University, USA*
Professor Tadao Kagono, *Japan Advanced Institute of Science and Technology*
Professor Gianni Lorenzoni, *University of Bologna, Italy*
Professor Leif Melin, *Jönköping International Business School, Sweden*
Professor Hans Pennings, *The Wharton School, University of Pennsylvania, USA*
Dr Martyn Pitt, *School of Business and Management, Brunel University, UK*
Professor Alan Rugman, *Kelly School of Business, Indiana University, USA*
Professor Joachim Schwalbach, *Humboldt-Universität zu Berlin, Germany*
Professor Jörg Sydow, *Freie Universität Berlin, Germany*

Contents

To Ody, Yali and Danielle

Preface

This book addresses an important question for managers: why don't best practices spread within organizations? Although the question is simple, the answer is not. As I will show, the transfer of practices is a complex phenomenon, with nuances that yield only to careful scrutiny. My findings concerning impediments to the transfer of best practices run counter to accepted wisdom. Several years after my first analysis, the initial findings have been independently corroborated by other researchers who study knowledge transfer as well as by the experience of many companies.

Perhaps the seminal moment for this book dates back to a now distant day in July 1994 when I entered the office of my thesis advisor with an almost complete dissertation. I had written up my methodology and presented the results that I had obtained. These were what one would consider strong results and therefore good news. Most of the other chapters of the thesis had already been fairly well developed (or so I'd thought), and thus I saw myself close to that moment where the advisor tells you to 'bind it' and prepare the document for the final sign-off. That is, I thought I was about a mere month away from the bliss of having completed my dissertation and obtaining my degree. I was in for a surprise.

My advisor looked briefly at the bulky report – over 100 pages of text, tables and graphics. He had an idea that the results were strong – we had had numerous previous brief exchanges and countless drafts prior to that moment. He knew how long and how hard I'd worked to get to that point. And he had already a fair sense of the nature of the results. Yet, he asked me to sit down. Once I sat he said: 'It is certainly clear that you have worked hard to obtain these data, when you did your fieldwork, when you customized this complex questionnaire, and it is clear also that the results that you are now showing to me are convincing and strong.'

He then paused and directed a penetrating look at me, asking pointedly: 'So what? What should I do differently as a researcher because of your findings? What should managers do differently because of your findings? So what?'

Not that I had neglected that question. Indeed, I thought that I had given it sufficient attention by speculating on what specific findings meant for research and for managers. Thus, for example, I noted that the quality of the relationship between the source and the recipient appeared to be an important factor, which meant that more attention should be paid to social ties in knowledge transfer research and that managers should allocate time and resources to develop those ties. These and other observations were recorded in a draft of the 'implications' chapter.

My advisor remained unimpressed. He indicated that the thesis seemed complete and met minimal quality standards, but that it still did not meet his expectations: 'You have certainly worked hard and by now have all the ingredients for a perfectly adequate dissertation. However, until you have answered satisfactorily the so-what question, you have not fully met my standards.' At that moment, I realized that the final chapter of the thesis was still incomplete and had to be re-written. As it was now evident to me, the contents of that chapter were, for my advisor, the litmus test for the quality of the work.

His reaction made me pause and ask (again) the so-what question, this time after I had completed everything else. Because one never knows what one is going to find before one actually finds it, the challenges of conducting the study, formulating the question, obtaining access to corporations, collecting the information and then processing it have to be confronted and resolved successfully before I could engage my imagination in earnest on the so-what question. And one may not realize the meaning of the findings for some time after. Indeed, seven months after I entered my advisor's office – not just one month as I was anticipating – I finally was able to articulate conclusions of convincing strength.

My new answer to the so-what question was both simpler and more profound. It crystallized once I could take a step back and 'see' the pattern painted by the results. Simply put, the pattern suggested that knowledge barriers, barriers that could only be understood in light of recent conceptual advances, were as important as motivation barriers. These findings suggested a rich set of additional explanatory factors for knowledge transfer researchers. They also suggested additional levers to overcome stickiness for managers; i.e., instead of devising increasingly complicated incentive systems, managers could alternatively explore ways to mitigate knowledge barriers.

Time has revealed how those implications would play out in practice. My peers have accepted the results and used them to inform their own research. Scholars in the fledgeing knowledge tradition have accepted me as one of them. Companies have altered some of their knowledge-management practices based on the findings. Texas Instruments, Chevron Corporation, American Productivity and Quality Center, EDS, Rank Xerox and Harris Corporation have both adopted and adapted some of the research learning. Numerous reviews have been written about it and about some of the articles that came from it. Consulting firms have used the research as a blueprint to construct their own. The thesis has been selected for the Free Press award for the dissertation competition and its methodology highlighted as particularly promising for the field of Strategic Management.

This recognition, together with the unwavering support and enthusiasm of Robb Grant, Charles Badden-Fuller, Rosemarie Nixon, Kiren Shoman and the Sage staff, and the able help of Rossella Cappetta (now a co-author), Catherine Dykes and Joanna Fueyo, gave me the courage and helped me sustain the impetus while I wrote and revised the book. To my dissertation, I have added in-depth examples, an updated summary and a more elaborated interpretation of the findings. I also describe in considerable detail how I have obtained them.

This book is the fruit of an intellectual journey that had many patrons. I would like to thank my mentor and colleague Sidney G. Winter for an enlightening intellectual journey into the world of routines and replication, as well as Linda Argote, Ned Bowman, Jean Paul McDuffie, Eric von Hippel, Bruce Kogut, Dan Levinthal, Harbir Singh and my dissertation committee, Sumantra Ghoshal, Michael Brimm, Karel Cool and Richard Rumelt. I would also like to acknowledge the crucial support of George Day, Gareth Dyas, Carla O'Dell, Jackson Grayson and Carlos Schmerkin.

1

Introduction

You can see a high-performance factory or office, but it just doesn't spread. I don't know why.

William Buehler, Senior Vice-President at Xerox

Mr Buehler's observation (Jacob, 1992) is a contemporary expression of an old puzzle – one that hasn't yet been resolved. Indeed, organizations often do not have to look too far to find best practices. In many cases, they find stellar performance in their own backyard. It seems sensible to expect that in-house examples will diffuse to other units of the organization, once uncovered. Peers will imitate and management will 'suggest'. Yet, evidence shows otherwise. Best practices do not readily spread within firms.

One reason for this might be that companies simply do not attempt to spread best practices. Incentives to search for better practices inside the firm may be limited because, in the absence of compelling evidence, comparable operations are expected to have equivalent performance. For example, similar semiconductor plants – with comparable equipment, personnel and technology – are mostly expected to yield similar productivity and quality. Thus, organizations with multi-plant or multi-office structures see themselves as homogeneous collections of similar units and, understandably, turn outside for inspiration.

Even when internal results clearly stand out, limited understanding of the underlying processes and lack of adequate measures make it laborious, uncertain and generally unfruitful to advocate the transfer of those practices to other sub-units of the organization. Without timely, detailed and comparable measures of operational performance (Jacob, 1992; Kaplan, 1990), the economic magnitude of gaps in operational performance can easily be dismissed as exaggerated, manipulative, or as the inescapable consequence of structural, unconquerable factors (Chew *et al.*, 1990; Hayes and Clark, 1985). Thus, when the tangible trauma of change is pitted against speculative benefits, efforts to identify and replicate superior practices within firms are frequently relegated to the category of 'important but not urgent'.

This reality has been slowly changing. Fact-based management techniques brought by total quality programmes (Crosby, 1984; Ishikawa, 1985; Juran, 1988), benchmarking initiatives (Camp, 1989) and re-engineering

(Hammer and Champy, 1993) have improved dramatically the understanding of internal operations and the availability of fine-grained measures of operational performance. Timely collection, dissemination and use of the information generated from these measures is now possible with reasonable effort, thanks to advances in information systems, e.g. intranets, data warehouses, decision support tools, ERP systems and group-ware. Gaps of 200 per cent or more in the performance of comparable units[1] – gaps worth several million dollars (Chew *et al.*, 1990) – are frequently found. The prospect of financial gains of that magnitude naturally triggers efforts to narrow these performance differentials.

For these reasons, a large number of organizations are now attempting to transfer best practices, to close internal performance gaps, to stop re-inventing the wheel and to eliminate deficiencies in performance. The rise of the knowledge economy has helped organizations recognize that knowledge assets are rapidly becoming their most precious source of competitive advantage, and that learning to better manage those assets has become a competitive necessity. Accordingly, it is increasingly common to find executive positions, such as Chief Knowledge Officer or Chief Learning Officer, that have the explicit mandate to transfer existing knowledge to other parts of the organization.

Yet, even though more attention is being directed to best practices, these remain stubbornly immobile. In a survey of 431 US and European organizations conducted in 1997 by Ernst & Young, only 14 per cent of the respondents judged satisfactory the performance of their organization in transferring existing knowledge internally. The remaining 86 per cent found it lacking (Ruggles, 1998). Another survey of 79 subsidiary presidents and their immediate superiors of three global Fortune 500 corporations found big gaps between expectations, perceptions and reality. Whereas the parent company expected 95 per cent of the subsidiaries to be actively sharing knowledge and perceived that about 89 per cent were actually doing so, in reality only 62 per cent were actively engaged in knowledge-sharing activities (Gupta and Govindarajan, 2000). Best practices are unlikely to spread if companies do not try to spread them. However, even when they do try to spread them, best practices spread less than expected, because transferring them effectively is often found to be far more difficult than expected. Transfers of practices within the firm tend to be 'sticky'.

This book

Why don't best practices spread? Any progress that could be made in understanding and unlocking the puzzle will have implications for strategic management, organizational theory and ultimately for society at large. That is because the notion of stickiness is related to fundamental questions such as why and when a firm may be superior to a market in creating and transferring knowledge, how organizations learn to derive competitive advantage from their knowledge resources and the general societal concern of how to better utilize existing knowledge assets. Thus, for example, understanding stickiness could help us better appreciate the workings of organizational flexibility, the potential value of acquisitions, the chances for success of strategic alliances, technology partnerships and technology transfer agreements and, more broadly, how organizations leverage their knowledge.

It is thus not surprising that the best-practices puzzle, articulated more than three decades ago by Dick Walton from the Harvard Business School, emerged as one of the most important managerial challenges of the late 1990s and remains high in the priority list of the new millennium (see, for example, Cairncross, 2000; Slywotzky and Morrison, 2000; Stewart, 2000).

This book is a close and careful look at the best-practices puzzle. You will find an in-depth look at transfers of best practices, a detailed exploration of the nature of the difficulties that might be encountered, of the factors that may underlie those difficulties and of some of the possible explanations for the puzzle that those factors suggest. Both qualitative and quantitative methods were used to understand the puzzle and look for possible ways to explain its persistence.

The persistence of the best-practice puzzle is in itself puzzling because the observation that it is difficult to transfer best practices is hardly a new discovery. Indeed, implementing internal transfers of best practice – of a superior technology or of a better way to organize work – have long been recognized as an important managerial challenge. As early as 1913, Ford transformed its entire operation from craft to assembly-line production (Hounshell, 1984). Toyota diffused the *kanban* system throughout the company (Ohno, 1978). Yet, in both cases, competitors encountered great difficulties in imitating these practices. Outside the automobile industry, there were public attempts to replicate exceptional manufacturing practices from DEC's Enfield factory, GE's Bromount factory and Westinghouse's College Station factory (Ulrich and Lake, 1990).[2]

The puzzle may persist because factors that could be grouped under the rubric of motivational barriers are typically the only ones blamed for the lack of diffusion of practices. Difficulties to the transfer of best practices within firms are traditionally ascribed to interdivisional jealousy, lack of incentives, lack of confidence, insufficient priority, lack of buy-in, a heavy inclination to re-invent the wheel or to plough twice the same fields, refusal of recipients to do exactly what they are told, resistance to change, lack of commitment, turf protection and many other manifestations of what seem to be part of the popular definition of the Not-Invented-Here or NIH syndrome.

Researchers who have looked at the phenomenon seem to agree. For example, Michael Porter notes that 'the mere hope that one business unit might learn something useful from another is frequently a hope not realized' (1985: 352). He explains that '[b]usiness units acting independently simply do not have the same incentives to propose and advocate strategies based on interrelationship as do higher level managers with a broader perspective'. He blames both the recipient, who can 'rarely be expected to seek out know-how elsewhere in the firm', and also the source, who 'will have little incentive to transfer [its know-how], particularly if it involves the time of some of their best people or involves proprietary technology that might leak out' (1985:368).

When difficulties are primarily pinned down on motivational factors, adequate incentives appear indispensable. For example, Porter argues that '[u]nless the motivation system reflects ... differences [in perspective], it will be extremely difficult to get business units to agree to pursue an interrelationship and to work together to implement it successfully. Instead they become embroiled in fruitless negotiations over the allocation of shared costs or over procedures for sharing revenue' (1985:386). In the same vein, Goold *et al.* (1994) note that enlightened, self-interested business unit managers will exert their implicit veto rights on opportunities for knowledge sharing that they personally find unattractive. Thus, overcoming difficulty is tantamount to convincing those business unit managers.

Approaching transfers of knowledge with such an exclusive focus on incentives immediately directs attention to transfer-related benefits that are or appear asymmetric, and to corporate incentive schemes that, by not offering any specific incentive to transfer, indirectly penalize managers who incur costs in supporting them. Corporate management is often reluctant to modify incentive systems because it fears that treating business units differently, or creating idiosyncratic measures of performance for each unit, will vastly complicate the management of the organization. That is because units that are sources of best practice might be able to excuse poor performance by citing their efforts to aid others. Thus, corporate management, rather than tinker with the organization's incentive system, prefers to leave the situation as it is. Maybe that's why the puzzle has persisted for such a long time.

In my quest to explore the best-practices puzzle, I have naturally considered the impact of motivational barriers, but did not stop there. Through a careful and extensive review of related literature and evidence on knowledge transfer and on how corporations use their knowledge assets, I discovered another set of reasons, besides incentives, that may explain why knowledge might not transfer.

I call this alternative set of reasons *knowledge barriers*. Examples of knowledge barriers are the recipient's level of knowledge prior to the transfer, how well the transferred practice is understood within the organization, the recipient's ability to unlearn, i.e. shed prior practices, and the pre-existing social ties between the source and the recipient of knowledge. These factors are qualitatively different from motivational barriers, such as the motivation of a source to share knowledge or to support the transfer of that knowledge and the motivation of a recipient to absorb and institutionalize external knowledge.

When motivational and knowledge barriers are both taken into consideration, a different picture emerges. Indeed, I've found that knowledge barriers could overshadow motivation barriers to the transfer of best practices within the firm, a discovery that has far-reaching implications for those who grapple daily with the best-practices puzzle and seek effective ways to enhance best-practice sharing and the use of existing knowledge within their organization. That is because it seems that it might be possible to design several alternative ways to enable knowledge sharing that do not require any modification to the incentive system and thus could be implemented within the existing organizational structure.

That basic picture can be elaborated further by taking into account the different stages that typify the evolution of a transfer. When I did that, I discovered that the relative importance of each type of barrier changed with the stage of the transfer, again highlighting non-obvious dynamics (e.g. that a motivated recipient could actually cause difficulties to transfer knowledge) and areas for future research. A more nuanced picture of the transfer suggests opportunities for sophisticated managerial interventions.

In sum, this book is a careful and detailed exploration of the best-practices puzzle. In the first part of the book, I discuss how I have approached the study of the puzzle, i.e. I define stickiness, describe the kinds of stickiness that one might consider and what kind of barriers one might expect. I then show both qualitative and quantitative evidence of stickiness and of its predictors, and discuss the implications that these findings may have for both research and practice. To help the reader further interpret the evidence I provide, I have included abundant detail of the methods that I have used to conduct this research.

I embarked in this quest because I was really intrigued by the persistence of the best-practices puzzle, by the seemingly limited effectiveness of conventional remedies and by what that implied about an organization's true ability to leverage existing knowledge. I attempted to go beyond just trying to provide one more key to unlock the one and only known gate to the effective transfer of best practices. I sought alternative gates. I believe that I have found some non-obvious ones, a discovery that in turn opens exciting alternative ways to leverage knowledge within the firm.

Organization of the book

Because the topic of this book speaks to a variety of practical and academic concerns, I structured the book so that it could be conveniently accessed by different readers, both by those with an academic orientation and by those with a practical one. For this reason, the main topics, ideas, findings and conclusions are covered in a relatively brief and accessible format in the main body of the book, which is followed, in technical appendices, with abundant detail about methods.

Thus a reader with practical preoccupations may read Chapter 2 for definitions, and then turn immediately to Chapter 7 for an overview of the findings, referring back to Chapters 4 and 5 to fill in details, to Chapter 6 for concrete examples and to Chapter 8 to read about the practical implications of the findings. This will give a practically minded reader enough familiarity with the topic to begin to relate the contents of the book to a specific situation, or perhaps to begin to sketch possible alternative courses of action.

Practical implications could be made much more detailed and specific by collecting and analysing information from a given situation. Such an in-depth quest will require a more careful reading of Chapter 4, which provides a conceptual discussion of the different barriers to knowledge transfer. The technical appendices contain tools that can be used to measure those barriers. In particular, the appendices contain an elaborate questionnaire with measures for each of the barriers, as well as for many other aspects of the transfer that could help paint a rather comprehensive picture of the transfer situation. Information collected with those tools could be then used to find out what happened in a particular instance or to inform an effort to identify and preempt difficulties.

The technical appendices, besides data collection tools, include a detailed exposition of the research methods as well as additional detail on the statistical findings. Those interested in researching knowledge within organizations may find in the appendices a description of special challenges that emerge in this kind of research and of how some of those challenges were met in this particular study.

Several other aspects of the book, besides the technical appendices, should be particularly appealing to graduate students. For example, Chapter 3 positions knowledge transfer within the concerns of strategic management. Further, the text offers a rather comprehensive review of relevant literature, especially in Chapters 4 and 5. In addition, for those interested in stickiness research, Chapter 8 offers a number of research implications, and sketches possible avenues for further research.

Finally, teachers both at the graduate and the undergraduate level may find that the book provides a general introduction to knowledge transfer for their students. Furthermore, parts of the book could prove to be useful additions to courses that span a variety of knowledge-related topics, such as knowledge management, organizational learning, benchmarking and the sharing of best practice.

In the end, I realize that each reader's needs are in some sense unique and could span a broad range of interests. Thus, rather than speculating further about different strategies for reading the book, I give below a brief description of the contents of each chapter to help the reader tailor his or her approach to specific concerns, angles, questions and interests.

In *Chapter 2*, I argue that the transfer of knowledge within the firm can be difficult. I then define the notion of stickiness as the difficulty to transfer knowledge and discuss how one could detect the existence of stickiness.

Chapter 3 positions the transfer of knowledge within the field of strategic management. The thesis of this chapter is that stickiness reflects the presence of internal factors that impede the realization of competitive advantage. It is claimed that stickiness hinders the appropriation of rents from existing knowledge assets. This in turn suggests that factors that cause stickiness act as internal barriers to rent appropriation.

Chapter 4 offers a typology of predictors of stickiness. Stickiness can be predicted by analysing properties of the transfer. In general, the unfolding of the transfer depends to some extent on the disposition and ability of the source and recipient, on the strength of the tie between them and on the characteristics of the object that is being re-created. The features of the organizational context where re-creation occurs are important as well. The impact of these factors is analysed in this chapter.

Chapter 5 offers a typology of stickiness. Four transfer phases are synthesized from the literature on knowledge transfer: initiation, implementation, ramp-up and integration. Each of these four phases can be difficult in a different way. Accordingly, I distinguish between four types of stickiness: initiation stickiness, implementation stickiness, ramp-up stickiness and integration stickiness. The nature of difficulty at each stage and possible predictors are discussed.

Chapter 6 illustrates the four types of stickiness – initiation, implementation, ramp-up and integration – with findings from in-depth fieldwork in three different companies. Initiation stickiness is illustrated with Rank Xerox's difficulties to initiate transfers between its European subsidiaries. Implementation and ramp-up stickiness are illustrated with Banc One's difficulties experienced when converting acquired banks. Integration stickiness is illustrated by Centel's difficulties to sustain in each of its divisions a 'best' practice that had already been effectively implemented.

Chapter 7 presents the results of statistical analysis aimed at identifying which were the best predictors of difficulty for each stage of the transfer and overall for the transfers of this study.

Chapter 8 suggests some implications of this study for further research on stickiness and for the practice of knowledge transfer. The chapter discusses the contributions to extant research on stickiness, which include a typology of stickiness as well as alternative ways to measure stickiness. The discussion of implications for research ends with suggestions for more specialized research on stickiness and on its antecedents. The development of implications for practice includes speculation about possible actions that could be taken to facilitate each stage of the transfer. Next, practical questions that typically arise during the initiation of knowledge transfer are addressed using data collected in this study. This includes the question of who should be the first recipient of an internal best-practice transfer when there are several viable candidates to choose from. It also includes the examination of how senior management interventions could affect stickiness.

Chapter 9 provides a summary of the book, the underlying study, its findings and their significance for research. The chapter concludes by arguing that we now have new clues to rethink prevailing wisdom about why best practices may not spread. Conventional wisdom blames incentives, i.e. motivational barriers, almost exclusively. The findings, however, point to knowledge-related barriers, not just to motivation-related barriers, as an important culprit.

The book also contains five technical appendices with details of the study. These appendices contain the research design, the questionnaire used for Phase I, an example of a cover letter used inside the companies, a partial list of the practices studies and a full version of the questionnaire used in Phase II of the study.

In the next chapter, I expand on the best-practices puzzle and introduce the notion of stickiness.

Notes

1. Besides the published references, I've found up to 10:1 gaps in performance in otherwise comparable units, and gaps of 2:1 rather frequently. Personal communication with Robert Camp, a widely known benchmarking specialist from Xerox, confirmed that gaps of 200–300 per cent are a typical finding in internal benchmarking efforts.

2. Likewise the socio-technical literature describes numerous attempts to replicate novel ways of organizing work internally (Walton, 1975).

2

Stickiness, Best Practices and Knowledge Transfer

Transfer of knowledge within the firm

Sub-units of a firm may achieve superior results in many different ways. For example, best practices may result from R&D activities, process improvement projects (Adler, 1990), re-designed operations (Hammer and Champy, 1993) or from greenfield operations established to resolve problems encountered in existing plants (Kerwin and Woodruff, 1992; Ulrich and Lake, 1990:240; Walton, 1975). Best practices may develop also in units serving large and sophisticated lead markets or in units with privileged access to a highly skilled workforce (Bartlett and Ghoshal, 1989). Finally, best practices may develop through benchmarking (Camp, 1989), acquisitions (Haspeslagh and Jemison, 1991), joint ventures with possessors of superior skills (Brown and Reich, 1989) or by 'gleaning' skills from strategic alliance partners (Doz and Hamel, 1998; Hamel and Prahalad, 1988). Through these various mechanisms, superior productive knowledge comes into the firm.

Automobile manufacturing plants provide many well-known examples of the process of formation of best practices. One such example is General Motors' Saturn. Saturn is a greenfield, 'clean slate' initiative to manufacture and distribute small, high-quality cars set up in response to similar offerings from Japanese manufacturers (Kerwin and Woodruff, 1992). Another example is the NUMMI car-manufacturing plant in Fremont, California, fruit of a joint venture between GM and Toyota. NUMMI productivity is comparable to that of its sister plant in Takaoda, Japan and equal or better than that of most other GM plants. It is organized according to Japanese production management methods, similar to those used in Toyota's own factories, but relies on a predominantly American workforce (Brown and Reich, 1989). Other examples of the emergence of best practices in the automobile industry include Toyota's Koromo plant, birthplace of the 'just-in-time' manufacturing method (Ohno, 1978), and the Ford flywheel magneto assembling department, where mass-manufacturing methods were first introduced at Ford to replace craft-production methods (Hounshell, 1984).

Organizations can leverage best practices by re-using such valuable knowledge in other sub-units within the organization. For example, in 1994, Tom Engibous, the CEO of Texas Instruments (TI), decided to act upon the disparity in yields among various wafer fabrication sites. TI 'had pockets of mediocrity next door to world class' (O'Dell and Jackson Grayson, 1998:62). By sharing best practice among its 13 plants, TI gained US$ 1.5 billion in annual free wafer fabrication capacity without building additional wafer fabrication sites. Likewise, Chevron decided in the early 1990s to look inside the firm for superior process knowledge. By 1992, the company had developed a worldwide company summary of 'hard' (e.g. distillation of crude) and 'soft' (e.g. energy conservation) best practices, which saved the company tens of millions of dollars (O'Dell and Jackson Grayson, 1998:63–4). In another striking example, Rank Xerox identified and shared marketing best practices among its European subsidiaries, saving over $150 million in the first year of the initiative (Deutsch, 2000; *Financial Times*, 1997).

Not surprisingly, the potential benefits that could be gained by diffusing the practice internally are frequently factored explicitly in the justification for investing in the creation of new practices. For example, part of GM's rationale for its $5 billion Saturn investment in the 1980s was to create a successful prototype its other divisions could copy, and in turn GM adopted Saturn methods 'wholesale' at its Oldsmobile division (Kerwin and Woodruff, 1992). Similarly, TI anticipated potential gigantic savings when it set up to collect and share data about plant practices (O'Dell and C. Jackson Grayson, 1998:62).

In all the above examples of internal transfers of best practice, the intended recipients can potentially benefit from the source's superior knowledge because they perform tasks that are similar in some way to that performed by the source (Galbraith, 1990; Stalk *et al.*, 1992). For that reason, such transfers are more likely to be horizontal, peer-to-peer, rather than vertical, through different stages of the value chain. Instead of taking place between units situated at subsequent stages of the value chain (Porter, 1985), these transfers of knowledge are likely to pair source and recipient units that perform roughly similar activities in the value chain. On occasion, the source unit may be a corporate unit that has the explicit mandate to diffuse a practice throughout the organization. In both cases, a key distinguishing feature of these transfers is that the knowledge to be transferred exists already within the confines of the organization in a form that makes it amenable to re-use.

Whether or not practical knowledge may deserve the grand title of 'best practice' is frequently questioned. The above examples refer to practices that yield superior productivity growth or are otherwise at or close to a technological frontier. As O'Dell and Jackson Grayson point out, in a fast-paced world, best practice is a moving target and, even in a static world, the notion of 'best' remains situation specific. They acknowledge the existence of alternative adjectives such as 'better', 'exemplary' or 'successfully demonstrated' that could describe reality better but point out that none of them is commonly used. Some companies develop their own internal vocabulary to deal with this question. For example, Chevron recognizes four levels of best practices: 'Good Idea,' 'Good Practice,' 'Local Best Practice' and 'Industry Best Practice'. For Chevron, a best practice must have been proven valuable and may be applicable to others. Likewise O'Dell and Jackson Grayson define it as a practice that has produced outstanding results and could be adapted. The spirit of these two definitions points to the essence of the notion of best practice, to the notion that best practice is a relevant example that yields better results than any known alternative. This makes the underlying knowledge worthy of scrutiny for possible re-use, even when substantial costs and risks are factored in those considerations.

A possible solution to sidestep the hazards of invoking the adjective 'best' is to focus on the phenomenon called 'transfer of best practice within the firm' and interpret the notion 'best practice' to include all those practices that the firm actually attempts to transfer. The notion of practice, however, can be made slightly more precise by associating it with the organization's routine use of knowledge. Transfers of best practice thus become dyadic exchanges of organizational knowledge between a source and a recipient unit in which the characteristics of the source and of the recipient both matter. The word 'transfer' is used – instead of 'diffusion' – to emphasize that the movement of knowledge within the organization is a distinct experience, not a gradual process of dissemination.[1] Transfers of best practice provide a propitious setting to observe transfers of knowledge within organizations, and to examine stickiness in a practical setting.

Transfers of knowledge might be 'sticky', i.e. difficult

Traditionally, the difficulties of transferring knowledge within the firm have been slighted both in theory and in practice. In early studies of technological innovation, new technology is assumed to diffuse instantly across total capital (Nelson, 1981:1049). Similarly, in early studies of international and domestic transfers of technology the transmission of technologies between and within countries was assumed to be costless (Reddy and Zhao, 1990:298; Teece, 1977:242). In the world of practice, many corporations assign untested junior managers to transfer and replicate advanced manufacturing technology, expecting that these transfers will be relatively straightforward. As Galbraith found, 'managers, engineers, and operators alike acknowledged that their particular transfer was *far more complicated than originally imagined*' [italics added] (1990:68).

Indeed, the transfer of knowledge within the firm takes time, sometimes as much as three years, and incurs costs and uncertainty. Teece (1976) found that the resource cost of transferring the capability to manufacture a product or a process across international borders averaged 19 per cent of the total manufacturing project costs,[2] reaching 59 per cent in one of the 26 projects he studied. Likewise, Mansfield *et al.* (1983) found that the cost of technology transfer averaged about 20 per cent of the total costs of establishing

26 overseas plants (Reddy and Zhao, 1990). The dollar cost of transfer in Teece's study averaged roughly $1.2 million, reaching as high as $7.4 million. From his evidence, Teece concluded that 'there seems to be little room for the notion that transfer costs are zero, or very nearly so' (1976:45).

Furthermore, the success of a transfer is never guaranteed. In Teece's sample, out of the 26 transfers, one failed to match the quality of the output at the source unit, two failed to match the material efficiency of the source unit and six failed to match the labour productivity of the source unit. In Galbraith's (1990) sample, out of 32 intra-firm complex technology transfers, 50 per cent experienced severe productivity problems and 20 per cent ultimately failed to achieve profitability. Likewise, General Motors could not replicate the success of NUMMI, its joint venture with Toyota, in its Van Nuys plant in California (Brown and Reich, 1989), or foster the imitation of Saturn practices in the Oldsmobile division (Kerwin and Woodruff, 1992).

Stickiness

Major Hunter-Hunt let his emotion over the *stickiness* of the Treasury evaporate in a deep sigh.
C. Mackenzie, *Water on Brain*

He had not imagined ... that there was anything more in Billson's recalcitrance ... than his usual official *stickiness*.
N. Blake, *Minute for Murder*

The intense *stickiness* of the situation.
P.G. Wodehouse, *Spring Fever*

You do seem to have involved her in some sort of *stickiness*.
J.D. Macdonald, *Girl*

The adjective *sticky* has been used in many different ways to connote immobility, inertness and inimitability. In the strategy literature, sticky has been used as a synonym for inert (Porter, 1994) or difficult to imitate (Foss *et al.*, 1995). Macroeconomists use the term 'sticky price' to describe prices that are slow to adjust. In the lingo of Wall Street sticky means difficult to sell. Eric von Hippel (1994) defined stickiness as the incremental cost of transferring a given unit of information in a form usable by the recipient. By implication, sticky information is harder to move.

As von Hippel points out, stickiness is a function of multiple factors, including the nature of knowledge and the choices and attributes of its seekers and providers. Indeed, some knowledge is inherently difficult to transfer. For example, Doz (1994:11) reports that innovative consulting companies, such as McKinsey or Arthur D. Little, find it difficult to share the perpetually evolving learning of their consultants. They are uncertain about what is there to be shared and of how it should be shared. As he argues, this problem is also common in R&D-intensive companies.

Yet, even proven and well-defined knowledge can be difficult to transfer because favourable tendencies[3] propelling its diffusion are 'nullified and off-set by competing organizational dynamics' (Walton, 1975:3). For example, the failure to transfer GM's NUMMI practices to the Van Nuys plant is principally attributed to the opposition of the labour union (Brown and Reich, 1989), and the difficulty that GM experienced in transferring Saturn's practices to its other divisions is principally attributed to 'star-envy'. As Kerwin and Woodruff (1992:74) reported: 'Saturn's success [fostered] more resentment from other GM nameplates than imitation.' TI's greatest challenges to share knowledge were to motivate employees to accept one another's ideas and to recognize and understand how they've become so successful (O'Dell and Jackson Grayson, 1998:81). Likewise, Hayes and Clark (1985:168) found that a high-tech firm experienced 'organizational difficulties' in transferring engineering knowledge because the source plants desired to protect proprietary knowledge and because the recipient plants were reluctant to assimilate superior manufacturing technology if that technology was developed at another plant.

This invokes another perhaps less well-known meaning of stickiness. According to the *Oxford English Dictionary*, besides its most popular meaning as gluey, the word stickiness describes also social situations typi-fied by hesitancy, stubbornness, awkwardness and unpleasantness. In line with this second interpretation of the word stickiness, I use the notion of 'sticky transfers' to denote transfers where vigilance and effort are required to detect and overcome difficulty. While, in general, all transfers of knowledge require some degree of effort, some transfers require signifi-cantly more effort than others. Those that require more effort are said to be stickier.

Thus, not just the knowledge but also the actual transfer could be said to be sticky. Stickiness is an attribute of a particular transfer of knowledge, which reflects both the characteristics of the transfer situation as well as those of the knowledge being transferred. An eminently practical question, then, is how do we know that a transfer is or will be sticky, i.e. how do we detect stickiness?

Detecting stickiness

Memory is attention in past tense.
   Daniel Goleman, cited in Gilovich, 1991

In a difficult transfer, problems are likely to escalate. Whereas some of the transfer-related problems will be diagnosed easily and resolved routinely by those directly involved with the transfer, other problems transcend the resourcefulness of the organizational actor(s) who are normally affected by and routinely resolve transfer-related problems. This process of escalation is typical to help desks, where clerks deal with routine problems directly, but escalate, i.e. refer upwards, more complex ones (Pentland and Rueter, 1994). Likewise several cycles of over-selling, over-committing and under-performing are typically observed in complex administrative situations or large projects that experience difficulty before the highest-level authorities recognize, acknowledge and get involved. Lack of timely attention compounds the problems. As Levinthal and March point out, higher-level learning occurs only when this lower-level adaptation breaks down: 'Insofar as subordinates respond to individual customer complaints, bosses are less pressed to do so' (Levinthal and March, 1993:101).

Complex transfer problems are likely to require additional deliberation, recourse to non-standard skills, allocation of supplemental resources and escalation of transfer-related decisions to higher hierarchical levels for resolution. Actors whose attention would not have been normally required, such as senior managers or consultants, are likely to be involved in efforts to identify and resolve this more complex level of problem. These actors will become involved on an exceptional basis to expedite the identification of possible solutions and to enable and coordinate their implementation.

This more complex level of problem is likely to be noticed more broadly because it interrupts the assumed flow of the transfer (Zeigarnik, 1967). In other words, this kind of problem is more likely to exceed the base rate of eventfulness of a typical transfer and thus is more likely to be noticed against a background of otherwise ambiguous and inconsistent organizational reality. This kind of problem is more likely to create a distinct moment of difficulty in the transfer (Gilovich, 1991) and thus is more likely to contribute to the overall perception of difficulty and to the intensity of efforts exerted to resolve the problem (March and Simon, 1958). The assessment of the degree of difficulty experienced in a transfer is likely to reflect the number and intensity of those distinct moments of difficulty. Other things being equal, a transfer is more likely to be perceived as sticky when efforts to resolve transfer problems become noteworthy (Hoopes and Postrel, 1999).

Stickiness is thus reflected in the eventfulness of the transfer. Not all events are necessarily transfer related, but all will call attention to the transfer effort. The transfer is likely to be remembered as eventful.

In the next chapter, I elaborate on how stickiness may affect firm performance.

Notes

1. Although in many occasions the word 'diffusion' and the word 'transfer' are used interchangeably, there is a crucial distinction between them. The word diffusion is generally used in connection with dissemination phenomena in which attention focuses on the source and on a generic destination unit. In such cases, idiosyncratic differences between individual recipient units are per force relegated to a secondary role, if not downright ignored. In contrast, the word transfer is

typically associated with situations in which the unit of analysis is the dyad, and attention in the analysis spans also the characteristics of the recipient of knowledge. Consequently, the word transfer signals close attention to the individual character- istics of both the source and of the recipient of knowledge. Because it is a ground assumption of this study that the identities of both the source and the recipient of knowledge merit detailed examination to fully assess a process of transfer, and that seldom can a practice be merely borrowed but that, in contrast, it typically needs to be adapted to the idiosyncratic requirements of a recipient unit, the use of the word 'transfer' is believed to better capture the nature of the phenomena under study. In discussing intra-organizational situations of technology transfer, Leonard-Barton (1990b) makes a similar distinction between 'point-to-point transfer' versus 'diffusion'. And Galbraith (1990:70) notes that typically the transfer is a 'distinct experience, not a gradual process of diffusion'.

2. Teece (1976:36) defined technology transfer costs as the 'costs of transmitting and absorbing the relevant firm, system, and industry-specific knowledge to the extent that this is necessary for the effective transfer of the technology'. The total costs of a manufacturing project in Teece's study includes, in addition to the cost of transfer, the cost of all the other 'activities involved in establishing a plant abroad and bringing it on stream'.

3. Walton conjectured that most of us would expect that an organizational pattern that is working better than one it replaced will be 'recommended by superiors and emulated by peers' (Walton, 1975:3).

3

Stickiness and Firm Performance

The performance of a firm reflects its ability to re-use superior knowledge before competitors are able to reproduce it effectively. A firm is supposedly at an advantage relative to imitators because it has better access to templates or working examples of its own practices.

Both external and internal factors can potentially affect the ability of a firm to extract value from superior knowledge. External factors that retard imitation prolong the period of time where competitive advantage is sustained and can include the use of patents, secrecy and defensive organizational mechanisms.[1] Such barriers to imitation slow down the speed of imitation.

Even when there is no threat of imitation, however, hypothetical gains may never materialize because of the working of internal factors. Scholars interested in explaining firm performance have neglected, until recently, a detailed examination of such internal factors. Explanations for the persistence of superior performance have over time progressively narrowed their focus – starting from an industry level of analysis, moving to an intra-industry level of analysis, then to a firm level of analysis. Recently researchers have begun hinting at the internal workings of a firm as the next natural step to deepen our understanding of the persistence of competitive advantage.[2]

The thesis of this chapter is that stickiness reflects the presence of internal factors that impede the realization of competitive advantage. This argument is made more specific and precise by grounding it in the strategic management literature. In short, it is claimed that stickiness hinders the appropriation of rents from existing knowledge assets. This in turn suggests that factors that cause stickiness act as internal barriers to rent appropriation.

Internal impediments to value creation

From profits to rents

In the course of its short life, the field of Strategic Management has witnessed a succession of explanations for the persistence of supra-normal profits, or more simply put, of success (Rumelt *et al.*, 1990). All of these explanations – motivated by the empirical observation that, within an industry, some firms did consistently better than others – posited the existence of impediments to the elimination of abnormal returns. First, abnormal returns were seen to be sustained by the presence of entry barriers (Bain, 1956; see Gilbert, 1989 for a comprehensive review). Entry barriers gave sellers within an industry enduring power over price, allowing them to collusively restrict output and realize some degree of monopoly profits. Next, Caves and Porter (1977) proposed the concept of barriers to mobility, which act as barriers to entry that are specific to a group of firms within an industry, rather than to an entire industry. Protected by mobility barriers, members of a (strategic) industry group enjoyed persistent supra-normal profits as a collective entity. Finally, Rumelt (1984) argues that there is no theoretical reason to limit mobility barriers to groups of firms. He advanced the concept of isolating mechanisms to refer to 'phenomena that limit the ex-post equilibration of rents among individual firms'. Likewise, Porter (1985) advanced the concept of barriers to imitation, which he defined as those barriers that make imitation of a firm's generic strategy difficult; a definition later generalized by Reed and deFillippi (1990:94) as the 'restraining or obstructing imitation by imitators'. This succession of explanations for the persistence of supra-normal profits suggests an imagery of walls around an industry, which shrink until they surround only a single firm.

This procession of shrinking defences of supra-normal profits stimulated a re-examination of the sources of those profits, as well as efforts to conceptualize anew those profits. What explains a particular firm's performance? Its membership in an industry, or its idiosyncratic endowment of assets and capabilities? Empirical tests (Hansen and Wernerfelt, 1989; Henderson and Cockburn, 1994; McGahan and Porter, 1997; Rumelt, 1991) revealed that the 'firm effect' explains at least as much variance as the 'industry effect', confirming idiosyncratic firm differences as important determinants of performance. And as Rumelt explains, '[o]nce the source of high profits is located in the firm's resource bundle rather than in its membership in a collective, the appropriate profit concept is that of rent' (1987:141). This conceptual distinction is significant because rents, unlike profits, persist in competitive equilibrium.[3] This is in part due to the relationship between rents and scarcity, which, itself, is in flux congruous with that of competitive equilibrium. When assets are specialized to the needs of a firm, or when their use involves significant transaction costs, the rent on that factor is not logically or operationally separable from the profits of the firm (Rumelt, 1987:143), since the transaction costs are a source of scarcity.

The efforts to conceptualize the source of profits has yielded a distinction of the different types of scarcity rents that a firm may eventually realize from owning an asset. An asset may yield monopoly rents if the scarcity value of that asset results from its protection from market entry, over the value it would have had in an open market (Klein *et al.*, 1978). An asset may yield Ricardian rents if its scarcity value results from it being in fixed supply, provided that the rent commanded by this factor is insufficient to attract new resources to use (Rumelt, 1987:142). Alternatively, when a firm, given its asset endowment, may generate value from a resource in excess of the value that could be generated by the next best use of that resource, the resource is said to generate quasi-rents (Klein *et al.*, 1978) or Marshalian-Pareto rents (Rumelt, 1987), even if the resource is not intrinsically scarce. In this case the rents are firm-specific, and stem from the interdependence of the acquired asset with other scarce firm-specific factors with which the asset is combined (Conner, 1991:134–6). Finally, a firm may achieve entrepreneurial rents[4] if it discovers a combination of resources that generate a rent, when *a priori*, the rent-yielding potential of that particular combination was uncertain (Knight, 1921). In this case, scarcity results from proprietary access to the knowledge of that particular combination. Once the knowledge diffuses to other imitators – effectively becoming public – the ability of the entrepreneur to earn rents from that particular combination of resources erodes (Arrow, 1962b; Schoemaker, 1990). In sum, monopoly rents, Ricardian rents, quasi-rents and entrepreneurial rents result from different classes of scarcity.[5]

Value creation as resource accumulation and rent appropriation

Because the profits realized by the firm originate in some form of scarcity, in the resource-based theory the profit maximizing firm is seen as seeker of scarce, valuable and costly-to-copy inputs for production and distribution (Conner, 1991; Grant, 1996). By accumulating resources with rent-yielding potential the firm may increase the amount of rents generated, and subsequently profits. Rumelt argues that accumulation of resources results essentially from 'profit seeking through corporate entrepreneurship which is intimately connected with the appearance and adjustment of unique and idiosyncratic resources' (1984:560). Thus, the resource accumulation process is seen as a manifestation of innovative or entrepreneurial activity. Profits can only result from this activity if the cost of accumulating the resources is lower than the rents these resources can actually produce (Peteraf, 1993). Lower costs may be the result of luck or they may be the result of foresight in acquiring undervalued resources, which are likely to originate from a firm's improved understanding of its own existing capabilities (Barney, 1986).

Unfortunately, acquiring undervalued resources is not enough. To realize the rent-yielding potential of such resources, the firm needs also to be able to appropriate the rents that the acquired resources may generate. In other words, to realize superior profits, the firm should be able not only to innovate, but also to appropriate rents from innovation. Thus innovation and rent appropriation have emerged as a main focus of researchers espousing the resource of the firm (Nelson, 1991) and its dynamic capabilities (Dosi *et al.*, 2000; Teece *et al.*, 1997).

Successful innovative activities generate valuable new assets, such as knowledge and competence (Winter, 1987). For example, valuable new knowledge may result from the firm's R&D activities, and new competencies may result from the firm's current manufacturing activities (Cohen and Levinthal, 1990; Nelson and Winter, 1982). A firm's knowledge base may also increase through externally focused formal search procedures (Teece *et al.*, 1990; von Hippel, 1988). One example of such an externally oriented procedure is competitive benchmarking (Camp, 1989), where firms seek to improve productivity by learning from the best-practice firms.[6] The firm may also increase its knowledge base through the generation of new applications from existing knowledge within the firm (Garud and Nayyar, 1994; Henderson and Clark, 1990; Kogut and Zander, 1992:391). Research and development, externally oriented search procedures such as competitive benchmarking, and new combinations of existing knowledge all add to the stock of rent-yielding assets of the firm.

A firm will realize above-average profits from its superior asset endowment only if it can generate all rents by deploying these assets efficiently and judiciously, and by holding the rents generated. A firm may fail to hold the rents because rents, once generated, are expropriated by powerful stakeholders, such as top management and other key employees (Klein *et al.*, 1978). A firm may spoil the rent-yielding potential of scarce assets because the decision of how to deploy those assets, which provides a ceiling for the profit that can be generated from them, is injudicious (Hill, 1992; Teece, 1987). The deployment decision might be injudicious because managers ordinarily make deployment decisions of strategic assets in a setting that is characterized by uncertainty, complexity and intra-organizational conflict (Amit and Schoemaker, 1993). Finally, a firm may dissipate part or all of the rent-yielding potential of its superior assets during the process of asset deployment (Ghemawat, 1991; Williamson, 1985). Thus, a superior asset endowment may not necessarily convert to rents because injudicious deployment, delay or slack sabotages efforts to appropriate rents.

Appropriating rents through intra-firm transfer of practices

The transfer of practice within the firm could be seen as a particular kind of knowledge transfer that enhances the appropriation of rents from the firm's existing stock of knowledge, since practice is a manifestation of the firm's knowledge. When the diffusion and incorporation of practices is incomplete, valuable knowledge may not be fully utilized in all parts of the firm. Consequently, the areas of the firm to which best practice has not yet diffused will exhibit deficits in performance that could have been avoided; this is referred to as 'organizational slack'. The transfer of practices can help reduce such deficits in performance.

When the details of a working example are accessible to the agent seeking to reproduce results, the process of transferring knowledge that underlies the superior results could be conceived as the replication of the firm's routines (Nelson and Winter, 1982; Rivkin, 2000). Replication differs from imitation in that the replicating agent has access to a template or working example of the practice to be replicated. The replicating agent seeks to obtain similar results by creating an exact or partial replica of a web of coordinating relationships connecting specific resources, so that a different but similar set of resources is coordinated by a very similar web of relationships (Winter, 1995).

The transfer of practices within the firm could be seen as a mechanism to reduce organizational slack because it reduces avoidable deficits in performance by reproducing superior outcomes throughout the firm.

Practice as manifestation of knowledge

Practice is a manifestation of organizational capability and is therefore embedded in organizational routines (Nelson and Winter, 1982). Practice is defined as what organizational members actually do. The expression 'organizational member' is used to define a unit that can 'accomplish something on its own' (Nelson and Winter, 1982:98). Following Nelson and Winter, organizational unit is used mostly to mean an individual. However, as they add, 'it is sometimes convenient to think of an organizational sub-unit as a "member" of the larger organization'. The expression 'actually do' is necessary to differentiate *actual* routine practice from what organizational members are *supposed* to be doing, as detailed in a formal description of their roles or 'nominal standards of the organization' (1982:108). For it is what organizational members actually do that determines organizational capability and, ultimately, the performance of the organization.

Organizational capability emerges over time through a process of organizational learning (Levitt and March, 1988). During this learning process, evolving productive knowledge embedded in individual skills and in technological artifacts is increasingly better coordinated through complex and partially tacit social arrangements, yielding smoother and more productive collective practices. Such a combination of productive knowledge or 'ingredients' and of coordination 'recipes' is referred to as an organizational routine (Nelson and Winter, 1982). Because the productivity of an organization increases with accumulated experience, organizations are said to learn those routines by doing (Arrow, 1962a; Yelle, 1979). Preserving the human skills and the socially embedded coordination recipes requires repetition. Recent research has demonstrated that when practice stops, organizational learning depreciates – sometimes rather fast (Argote, 1999; Argote *et al.*, 1990; Darr *et al.*, 1995). Thus, organizations not only learn by doing but also remember by doing, and thus routines act as the memory for the organization's knowledge. Practice is seen as fragmented, distributed and embedded in organizational routines. Thus practice may be seen as a manifestation of organizational knowledge.

Intra-firm heterogeneity and organizational slack

Imagine a large, multi-unit firm. Further, imagine that all the units in that firm produce essentially the same product or service with the same underlying technology. If all units within the firm are equally productive we may say that along this dimension, i.e. productivity, the firm is internally homogeneous. There is intra-firm homogeneity. Conversely, imagine that despite producing essentially the same products or services with the same underlying technology, there is significant variation in productivity among the different units. In this latter case, it can be said that, productivity-wise, the firm is internally heterogeneous.[7] That is, there exists *intra-firm heterogeneity*.

Intra-firm heterogeneity within multi-unit firms has long been known to exist. Among the first to call attention to such a phenomenon was Leibenstein who disputed the assumption, then common in economic studies, that 'every firm purchases and utilizes all of its inputs "efficiently" ' (1966:397)[8] – see also Frantz (1988). Based on evidence he himself collected, Leibenstein argued that there seemed to be a 'great deal of possible variation in output for similar amounts of capital and labor and for similar techniques ... [i.e.] similar types of equipment' (1966:404). Thus he concluded that inefficiency in acquiring and utilizing input resources, which he called 'X-inefficiency', was pervasive. Stalk and Hout (1990) made a similar discovery. In 1979 they were startled by data provided by a client who had benchmarked the performance of his key factories, discovering sizable differences in productivity among what were considered up until that point comparable plants. Over the years they found many more examples of similar gaps in performance among units of multi-plant firms. More recently Chew, Bresnahan and Clark collected more systematic evidence of intra-firm heterogeneity:[9]

> During the past several years, we and our colleagues have studied productivity of multiplant firms in over two dozen widely different industries, involving plants engaged in discrete part production and process flow and in high-tech and low-tech operations. In every environment, the research has identified large differences in plant-to-plant productivity within the same firm, even when the plants employed similar technologies and produced similar, occasionally identical, product ... it was not uncommon to find 3 to 1 differences between the best and worst plants of a same firm. (Chew *et al.*, 1990:129)

There can be many reasons for the existence of intra-firm heterogeneity. One possible reason is that different sub-units face substantially different environmental demands. For example, the size of a sub-unit's local market and the characteristics of the local labour force might differ, their products may be modified to comply with local tastes, preferences and regulations, or some sub-units may face stiffer competition than others. A second possible reason for intra-firm heterogeneity is that although all sub-units employ the same underlying production technology, there may be some differences in the amount and the vintage of their equipment. Finally, a third possible reason for intra-firm heterogeneity might be the incomplete diffusion and incorporation of the organization's policies and practices in all parts of the organization (Pfeffer, 1982:184).

This last reason for intra-firm heterogeneity – incomplete diffusion and incorporation of organizational policies and practices in all parts of the organization – amounts to organizational slack. After controlling for environmentally induced differences and for equipment vintage differences, the residual variations in productivity could be significantly reduced, if not eliminated, by transferring relevant practices from the most productive units to the least productive ones. When this is done, as Leibenstein (1966) puts it, knowledge is used to capacity. Thus, if knowledge of how to be more productive is not diffused within the organization, rents accruing to existing knowledge within the firm are dissipated. These avoidable deficits in performance add up to organizational slack.

This, of course, invites the question of how important the residual variation in productivity is after controlling for environmental and technological variation. Leibenstein attributed most of the differences in performance to slack, although he did not control systematically for environmental or technological differences. In the Chew *et al.* study, differentials in productivity of 2:1 still remained even after controlling for differences in the age and size of plants, their technology and their location. Chew *et al.* estimated that bringing below-average plants up to average performance would increase total firm profits by over 20 per cent. They found it hard to believe that, once uncovered, such intra-firm productivity variations would be neglected for long.

If the residual can be so substantial, we may infer that in many cases the presence of intra-firm heterogeneity, as defined above, will be significantly correlated with the presence of organizational slack. What is more important, we can also infer that, in those cases, effective sharing of best practices within the firm can reduce organizational slack.

Transfer of best practice as a mechanism for reducing organizational slack

The following example illustrates the essence of how the transfer of best practice reduces organizational slack. Ponder Figure 3.1. The rectangle with rounded corners represents a firm composed of three roughly comparable manufacturing plants (the inner circles). A white circle represents standard manufacturing practice, which yields one unit of profits, a black circle represents best practice, which yields two units of profit. The numbers to the right of the circles represent the productivity of the corresponding plant.

In the left-hand rectangle the firm is perfectly homogeneous. All plants are equally productive. Each plant of the firm is as productive (productivity = 1)

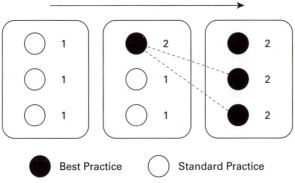

Figure 3.1 Reducing Organizational Slack

as the most productive of the firm's plant (productivity = 1). Consequently the firm is using available knowledge within the firm to full capacity. On this measure, organizational slack is zero, with respect to the internal production possibility frontier.

In the central rectangle, one plant of this previously homogeneous firm acquires new knowledge[10] and thanks to this new knowledge becomes more productive (productivity = 2) than the other plants of the firm. Now, intra-firm heterogeneity has increased. And so has slack.[11] Slack in productivity has increased from zero to two, because two out of the three plants do not use the new knowledge.

In the right-hand rectangle, new knowledge has been replicated and put to use successfully in the other plants. Consequently, these plants have doubled their productivity and the total productivity of the firm will increase from four to six. Intra-firm heterogeneity has again vanished. Intra-firm transfer of best practice eliminated organizational slack, thus helping the firm realize all potential rents from the newly acquired knowledge.

Conclusion: stickiness hinders rent appropriation

Intra-firm transfer of best practice is thus a way to realize and appropriate rents by re-creating existing knowledge to replicate superior outcomes. Accordingly, stickiness hinders the appropriation of rents that could potentially be extracted from the existing stock of the firm's knowledge. The factors that cause stickiness represent *barriers to rent appropriation.*

In limiting intra-firm rent equilibration, barriers to appropriation play a role within firms analogous to that which isolating mechanisms[12] fulfil in limiting ex-post rent equilibration between firms. Thus barriers to appropriation act as intra-firm isolating mechanisms. Intra-firm isolating mechanisms reduce not only the imitability but also the mobility of the firm's knowledge (Chi, 1994). In their presence, knowledge is re-created only with difficulty and, consequently, practices within the firm will tend to persist in form and function,[13] i.e. practices will be inert and their transfer sticky (Rumelt, 1994). The more significant intra-firm isolating mechanisms are, the stickier transfers of knowledge within the firm will be.

Therefore, the presence of barriers to rent appropriation could be detected by monitoring the degree of difficulty experienced in re-creating organizational practices.

The next chapter introduces a conceptual framework to guide the empirical analysis of causes of stickiness.

Notes

1. See Levin *et al.* (1987); Rivkin (2001).
2. In an intriguing study, Dyer shows that a firm that uses identical suppliers as its competitors do and purchases similar inputs from the same supplier achieves competitive advantage through those suppliers because of the existence of intra-firm barriers to knowledge transfer within the supplier (Dyer, 2000).
3. Dierickx and Cool (1989:3) elaborate the consequences of failing to distinguish between profit and rent. Failure to identify the firm's real source of above-normal earnings may lead to hidden cross-subsidization which distort performance appraisal and capital allocation decisions; may lead the firm to use a scarce resource, thus possibly overlooking other more profitable alternatives for deployment; and finally may lead the firm to fail to protect scarce resources from erosion.
4. Also called Schumpeterian rents.
5. See Winter (1995) for a systematic classification of rents from efficiency-enhancing innovations.
6. See Slater (1993) for a discussion of the best-practice programme at General Electric.
7. Of course, this view of homogeneity and heterogeneity is not restricted to the function of production, but could be equally applicable to any business process that is common to many or all of the sub-units, e.g. marketing, sales, R&D.
8. This assumption had been earlier challenged by Hayek. He reminded economists '[how easy it is] for an inefficient manager to dissipate the differentials on which profitability rests, and that it is possible, with the same technical facilities, to produce with a greater variety of costs, [facts which] are among the commonplaces of business experience which do not seem to be equally familiar in the study of the economist' (Hayek, 1945, quoted in Williamson, 1985:8).
9. Besides the published references, personal communication with Robert Camp, a reputed benchmarking specialist from Xerox, confirmed that gaps of 200–300 per cent in the operational performance of comparable units is a typical finding in internal benchmarking efforts.
10. New knowledge could be brought from the outside by licensing a superior technology or by benchmarking with another firm. Alternatively it could be developed through internal R&D.
11. Assuming no significant environmental or technological differences.
12. Rumelt (1984).
13. Assuming away depreciation of knowledge.

4

Predictors of Stickiness

Stickiness can be predicted by analysing properties of the transfer. Traditional approaches to the re-creation of knowledge within organizations have paid little attention to impediments. For example, communication theory views the process as one where the source transmits a signal to the recipient – a process in which information transfer is almost instantaneous and costless (Shannon and Weaver, 1949).

Subsequent analysis of knowledge transfer has recognized some of the impediments to knowledge transfer that result from the cognitive and emotional characteristics of human beings, and the social systems they create. These include the limited information processing capacity of 'social channels' (Arrow, 1974), the emotions and experiences of sense-making individuals (Rogers, 1994), the peculiarities of the relationship and of the social context in which the transfer is embedded (Hansen, 1999; Kostova, 1999; Szulanski, 1996), distortions in the communication process (Putnam *et al.*, 1996; Stohl and Redding, 1987), and characteristics of the knowledge transferred (Kogut and Zander, 1992; Nelson and Winter, 1982; Winter, 1987). These features add numerous complications, which could, in many cases, transform the 'act' of transfer into an intricate process. Therefore, some degree of difficulty could be expected in most situations.

In general, the unfolding of the transfer depends to some extent on the disposition and ability of the source and recipient, on the strength of the tie between them, and on the characteristics of the object that is being re-created. The features of the organizational context where re-creation occurs are important as well.

Traditional analysis acknowledges these factors[1] but stops short of specifying their impact. This task is undertaken here.

Characteristics of knowledge and stickiness

Causal ambiguity

Successful replication of results, in a novel setting, may be compromised by idiosyncratic features of the new setting in which knowledge is used. The theory of uncertain imitability (Lippman and Rumelt, 1982; Rumelt, 1984) suggests that there may be irreducible uncertainty connected with the attempt to replicate results that is generated by re-creating knowledge and putting it to use. A completely successful re-creation of knowledge is impossible since there is irreducible uncertainty that prevents a complete understanding of how features of the new context affect the outcome of the re-creation effort. Modelling the replication of results as the re-creation of a production function, Lippman and Rumelt explain that uncertainty is most likely to result from ambiguity about what the factors of production are and how they interact during production. As Rumelt (1984:562) explicates, 'if the precise reasons for success or failure cannot be determined, even after the event has occurred, there is causal ambiguity and it is impossible to produce an unambiguous list of the factors of production, much less measure their marginal contribution'. Therefore, Rumelt (1984:567) concludes that in the pure theory of uncertain imitability, the fundamental factor that hinders the precise replication of results from the use of knowledge is causal ambiguity.[2]

Causal ambiguity increases stickiness; the process whereby this occurs is explained by Jensen and Meckling:

> Uncertainty about what specific piece of idiosyncratic knowledge is valuable enlarges transfer costs in a subtle way. After the fact, it is often obvious that a specific piece of knowledge critical to a decision could have been transferred at low cost (for example, particular quirks of an organization, person, legal rule, or custom). But transferring this specific piece of knowledge in advance requires knowing in advance that it will be critical. (1992:255)

Costly omissions are more likely when there is causal ambiguity.

Routinized use of causally ambiguous knowledge is often accompanied by gaps between formal and actual patterns of use. Brown and Duguid (1991:41), based on detailed ethnographic studies of service technicians, noted variance between formal descriptions of work contained in training programmes and manuals, and actual work practices as performed by the organization's members. Likewise, Nelson and Winter distinguished between 'nominal standards of the organization' (1982:108) and routine operation. Gaps between formal and actual patterns of use result from partial articulation of the espoused rules that govern behaviour (Argyris and Schon, 1978), because of the partly tacit nature of individual skills (Polanyi, 1962) and of the coordination principles that govern collective action (Kogut and Zander, 1992; Winter, 1987). Gaps between formal and actual patterns of use also arise because incomplete knowledge of the production process precludes effective management (Bohn, 1994), and because the organization is opaque to decision makers (Williamson, 1975). There is also a need to maintain a social truce to preserve routine operation (Nelson and Winter, 1982).

Essentially, more than absence of know-how, causal ambiguity signals the absence of knowledge as to why something is done ('know-why'), including why a given action results in a given outcome. If results cannot be precisely reproduced elsewhere because of differing environmental conditions, and if there are causal ambiguities about the inner workings of productive knowledge, then problems that arise in the new environment have to be solved *in situ* through costly trial and error. As Paul Adler (1990:951) explains, when highly technologically sophisticated process knowledge is transferred, 'its "reach" into poorly mastered process techniques is such that any substantial divergence of process designs risks multiplying operational problems beyond manageable levels'. Thus, the higher the causal ambiguity, the more difficult it may prove to replicate results from the use of knowledge. Consequently,

Hypothesis 1: *Ceteris paribus*, causal ambiguity is positively correlated with stickiness.

Unproven knowledge

When knowledge has been put to use for a brief period of time or on a limited scale or scope, the claim that the same knowledge will be effective in a new situation may be somewhat speculative, due to lack of sufficient empirical substantiation. This dearth of information may affect the expectations of potential recipients (Lenox, 1999), who may be more reluctant to engage in the re-creation of that knowledge (Rogers, 1983) and who will question controversial integration efforts (Goodman *et al.*, 1980; Nelson and Winter, 1982). Thus,

Hypothesis 2: *Ceteris paribus*, absence of proof of the usefulness of knowledge is positively correlated with stickiness.

Characteristics of source and stickiness

Source lacks motivation

A source's agent can assume two roles: it can act as gatekeeper to knowledge in use, or it can supply a conception of such knowledge. Direct observation of knowledge in use allows the recipient to infer quick and arbitrarily precise answers. However, inferences drawn from observation may exceed the scope of the original conception of the practice, leading to an overprescription of its functioning, and ultimately to the articulation of *de facto* solutions to as-of-yet unspecified problems (Brooks, 1995). Conversely, a supplied conception of the practice may leave out practical detail that is necessary for any viable re-creation.

Consequently, the motivation of the source of knowledge to supply conceptions of the practice or to facilitate access to the recipient may influence the degree of difficulty experienced during a re-creation effort. For example, the source may be reluctant to share crucial knowledge for fear of losing ownership (the 'Invented Here' or I.H. syndrome), or a position of privilege and superiority, which incorporates the fear of becoming dispensable, or resentful for lack of recognition of the hard work that led to success. Furthermore, and especially in the first moments of knowledge transfer, the source may have to make an enhanced effort to support the recipient. This effort may interfere with the source's ability to attend to its main mission, unless the mission is a part of the effort, which may lead to a decrease in motivation. Accordingly,

Hypothesis 3: *Ceteris paribus*, lack of motivation of the source is positively correlated with stickiness.

Source lacks credibility

The credibility of the source affects how the conception of the practice supplied by the source will influence the behaviour of the recipient. When the source is credible, i.e. perceived as knowledgeable and trustworthy, the recipient will be less suspicious of the offered conception and therefore more open and receptive to its detail (Hovland and Weiss, 1951; Hovland *et al.*, 1949). This outlook increases the amount of information that can be exchanged (Carley, 1991; Tsai and Ghoshal, 1998), as well as decreasing the cost of the exchange (Curall and Judge, 1995; Zaheer *et al.*, 1998). More detail can be communicated to the recipient, which can thus afford a better grasp of the source's conception of the practice. Credibility could thus reduce stickiness.

On the other hand, a credible source might distract the recipient from the details of the supplied conception of the practice, beyond a general impression of the source's idea (Allen and Stiff, 1989; Perry, 1996). As Petty and Cacioppo (1986) argue, a credible source inhibits critical thinking, i.e. the processing and counter-arguing that would normally take place during the receipt of a counter-attitudinal message. The recipient will expect little damage to ensue from interactions with a credible source (Noteboom *et al.*, 1997) and, consequently, will take fewer steps to reduce the inherent uncertainty of the situation by closely monitoring the actions of the source (Berber, 1983; Lewis and Weigert, 1985; McAllister, 1995).[3]

It is generally believed that the positive effects of credibility dominate the negative.[4] This concept originated from Aristotle's seminal observation that the opinions of 'good men' are more influential on others' behaviour – an observation that has received clear empirical support. This concept is illustrated by the results of experiments showing that immediately following a communication episode, a credible source substantially affects the recipient's attitude (Allen and Stiff, 1989; Capon and Hulbert, 1973; Hovland and Weiss, 1951; Hovland *et al.*, 1949; Kelman and Hovland, 1953; Perry, 1996). More generally, factors more traditionally associated with credibility, such as trustworthiness (Zaheer *et al.*, 1998), status (Benjamin and Podolny, 1999) and social capital (Belliveau *et al.*, 1996; Nahapiet and Ghoshal, 1998;

Tsai and Ghoshal, 1998) are believed to contribute to the efficiency of social exchange. Hence,

Hypothesis 4: *Ceteris paribus*, lack of credibility of the source is positively correlated with stickiness.

Characteristics of recipient and stickiness

Recipient lacks motivation

A recipient's motivation to accept knowledge from an external source, and to engage in the necessary activities to re-create and apply this knowledge, may prove critical to ensure a non-eventful replication. The reluctance of some recipients to accept knowledge from the outside (the 'Not Invented Here' or N.I.H. syndrome) is well documented (Hayes and Clark, 1985; Katz and Kahn, 1982). Lack of motivation may result in foot dragging, passivity, feigned acceptance, hidden sabotage or outright rejection in the implementation of new knowledge (Zaltman *et al.*, 1973). This resistance may manifest itself during every activity that the recipient performs to support the re-creation of knowledge, such as absorbing the source's understanding, analysing the feasibility of transfer, bridging the communication gap with the source unit, planning the transfer, implementing systems and facilities necessary for successful absorption of new knowledge, assigning personnel for education and training, and solving unexpected problems that stem from the utilization of new knowledge. Thus,

Hypothesis 5: *Ceteris paribus*, lack of motivation of the recipient is positively correlated with stickiness.

Recipient lacks absorptive capacity

The ability to exploit outside sources of knowledge is largely a function of the prior level of related knowledge (Cohen and Levinthal, 1989, 1990; Dewar and Dutton, 1986). At the most elementary level, this knowledge includes basic skills, a shared language, prior experience that is relevant, and up-to-date information on related knowledge domains (Cohen and Levinthal, 1990; Galbraith, 1990; Nord and Tucker, 1987; Pennings and Harianto, 1992a; Walton, 1975). Critical prior knowledge also includes an awareness of the locus of useful complementary expertise within and outside the organization. Examples of this awareness are knowledge of who knows what, who can help with what problem, or who can exploit new information (Cohen and Levinthal, 1990; Nord and Tucker, 1987; Pennings and Harianto 1992a, 1992b). The stock of prior-related knowledge determines the 'absorptive capacity' (Cohen and Levinthal, 1990:128) of a recipient of knowledge.[5]

A recipient that lacks absorptive capacity will be less likely to recognize the value of new knowledge, less likely to re-create that knowledge and less likely to apply it successfully. This may increase the cost, slow the completion and even compromise the success of a re-creation effort. Thus,

Hypothesis 6: *Ceteris paribus*, the lack of absorptive capacity of the recipient is positively correlated with stickiness.

Recipient lacks retentive capacity

A transfer of knowledge is successful if there is long-term retention of the transferred knowledge (Druckman and Bjork, 1991), i.e. to the extent that the recipient persists in using that knowledge when practicable (Glaser *et al.*, 1983; Kostova, 1999). Persistence is more likely when re-created knowledge continues to be used until it loses its novelty and becomes a fact, a part of the objective and of the reality of the recipient that is taken for granted (Rogers, 1983; Zucker, 1977). This is more likely when use of new knowledge is fully extended, and when specific steps are taken to eradicate old knowledge (Glaser *et al.*, 1983; Yin, 1979). Studies of innovation (Nord and Tucker, 1987; Rogers, 1983) and of the persistence of planned organizational change (Goodman and Associates, 1982; Yin, 1979; see Glaser *et al.*, 1983: 221–51 for a review) have documented instances where the use of superior technical and organizational knowledge is discontinued after successful implementation. The ability of a recipient to institutionalize the utilization of new knowledge is a reflection of its 'retentive capacity.' This capacity is tested when the difficulties initially experienced during the integration of re-created knowledge serve as excuses for the discontinuation of its use; when feasible, this can cause reversion to the status quo (Zaltman *et al.*, 1973). Consequently,

Hypothesis 7: *Ceteris paribus*, the lack of retentive capacity of a recipient is positively correlated with stickiness.

Characteristics of context and stickiness

Barren organizational context[6]

The organizational context may affect the gestation and evolution of an initiative to transfer. In an organizational context in which the development of a transfer seed is facilitated, the context could be considered 'fertile'. Yet, the same transfer seed that unfolds fully and grows well in one context may grow poorly and yield ephemeral results in another; moreover in a third context, this seed may remain totally unrecognized. Insofar as the context nurtures the development of a transfer seed, the gestation and evolution of the transfer resembles the germination of a seed. Conversely, a context where knowledge transfer seeds cannot grow could be said to be barren, since the seeds cannot grow and mature, which effectively precludes their transfer. Formal structure and systems of the organizational context

(Bower, 1970; Chakravarthy and Doz, 1992; Chew *et al.*, 1990; Hayes and Clark, 1985), sources of coordination and expertise (Argote *et al.*, 1990; Chew *et al.*, 1990) and behaviour-framing attributes (Ghoshal and Bartlett, 1994; Schein, 1985) can influence the number of attempts to re-create knowledge, as well as the outcome of those attempts. Consequently,

Hypothesis 8: *Ceteris paribus*, a barren organizational context is positively correlated with stickiness.

Arduous relationship between the source and the recipient

Another important contextual aspect for both the source and the recipient of knowledge is the nature of their pre-existing relationship. A transfer of knowledge is rarely a singular event, but more often it is an iterative exchange process. A potential recipient may require explanations of the nature of the knowledge being transferred to decide whether this knowledge would meet its needs. Likewise, once engaged in a transfer, the source may have to work to gain a closer appreciation of the needs of the recipient, in order to select appropriate components to transfer. Further, consideration of the source's unresolved problems may support the initial period of utilization. The success of this exchange depends to some extent on the strength of the tie (Hansen, 1999), which is detectable in the ease of communication (Arrow, 1974) and in the 'intimacy' of the relationship (Marsden, 1990). Intimacy to some extent reflects a shared appreciation of the meaning of theories, puzzles, measures and accepted results which are conditions that ease communication since messages can be thought of as selections from a predefined set (Boland and Tenkasi, 1995:355). Conversely, an arduous relationship might create additional hardships to the transfer of knowledge. Thus,

Hypothesis 9: *Ceteris paribus*, an arduous relationship between source and recipient is positively correlated with stickiness.

Notes

1. The mathematical theory of communication (Shannon and Weaver, 1949), the theoretical underpinning for the signalling metaphor, has been deemed the most important single stimulus for the development of other models and theories in communication (Serevin and Tankerd, 1988). It served as the 'paradigm for communication study, providing single, easily understandable specification of the main components of the communication act: source, message, channel, receiver' (Rogers, 1994:438). This theory has been the main reference in the study of knowledge transfer (Attewell, 1992).

2. Bohn (1994) has called causally ambiguous knowledge 'incomplete'. He suggested a practical definition of complete knowledge as a 'model that will predict output characteristics to an accuracy of one-tenth of the tolerance band, for changes in inputs across a 2:1 range, and including all interactions' (1974:70).

3. In particular, McAllister (1995) argues that a high level of cognition-based trust, that is the trust derived from the evaluation of the positive characteristics of

the other person, is associated with little control-based monitoring, that is the monitoring of the other person's actions in order to control her or him.

4. For individuals, credibility is largely a reflection of their expertise and trust-worthiness (Perloff, 1993; Sternthal *et al.*, 1978).

5. The notion of absorptive capacity has some similarity with the notion of decentration – a capacity to transcend the egocentric here-and-now by temporarily adopting the perspective of another person (Rommetveit, 1974:43–4).

6. This brief discussion of the organizational context is limited to an intra-firm setting.

5

Types of Stickiness

Introduction: a process approach to knowledge transfer

Further insight into stickiness can be gained by opening the 'black box' of a transfer and analysing the details of the process. Such a process approach to the study of a transfer is often distinguished from a results, event or variance approach (Mohr, 1982). The latter focuses on describing and explaining results. Process research focuses on actual sequences of events, stressing the decision process involved and the nature of implementation problems.

A rather common way to analyse the process of transfer consists of specifying a set of phases and demarcating milestones (Van de Ven, 1992). Current understanding of transfer processes provides grounds to specify four distinct stages of a transfer. A distinction is usually drawn between the initiation and the implementation of a transfer. Within the implementation phase, further distinctions are often made between (a) the initial implementation effort, (b) the ramp-up to satisfactory performance, and (c) subsequent follow-through and evaluation efforts to integrate the practice with other practices of the recipient. Initial implementation of a new practice and the subsequent ramp-up to satisfactory performance involve a two-step sequence of first 'learning before doing' (Pisano, 1996) – either by planning (Argote, 1999) or by experimenting in a contrived setting before knowledge is actually put to use by the recipient – and then 'learning by doing', which entails the resolution of unexpected problems that arise when new knowledge is put to use by the recipient (von Hippel and Tyre, 1995). Follow-through efforts typically aim at maintaining and improving the outcome of the transfer after satisfactory results are initially obtained.

Specific events may indicate the conclusion of a specific phase and the beginning of another. Possible milestones during the process of knowledge transfer are the formation of the transfer seed, the decision to transfer, start of utilization and the achievement of satisfactory performance. The resulting four-phase process model is depicted in Figure 5.1.

Specifying the milestones

Formation of the transfer seed. A transfer seed is formed as soon as a need and knowledge that if put to use could address that need co-exist within the

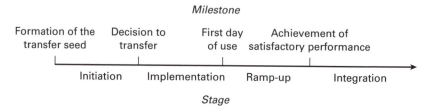

Figure 5.1

organization. Teece (1976:26) proposes that a transfer begins 'when a need or a potential is recognized'. Indeed, before a particular intra-firm transfer of knowledge can take place, the organizational participants need to be aware that this knowledge exists within the context of the organization, and they also need to be aware that it may be feasible to use this knowledge to address their needs. As Zaltman *et al.* (1973) point out, it is not clear whether the perception of a gap in performance initiates the process of search that results in the identification of potentially transferable knowledge or whether the opposite sequence actually holds, namely that the discovery of superior knowledge that could substantially impact a sub-unit's performance is what leads to the alteration of the expectations of the sub-unit; i.e. what was before considered satisfactory performance becomes, after the discovery of the new knowledge, unsatisfactory.[1]

Decision to transfer. This decision may be taken formally in a centralized, authoritative manner, or it may be spontaneous, informal and, in some cases, even unobservable. Teece (1976:27) observed that the transfer generally begins in earnest when a licence contract is signed or when 'the formal approval of the relevant executive group or groups is obtained'. Besides the signing of a formal document, the decision to transfer could be the outcome of a team meeting, a presentation to senior management or a simple handshake. An empirical surrogate to the decision to transfer is the beginning of any activity connected to the actual transfer, such as exchange of documents, capital resources, physical resources or human resources associated with the transfer of knowledge.

First day of use. This milestone marks the beginning of use of the new knowledge by the recipient. In Teece's study this milestone corresponds to the manufacturing 'start-up', i.e. bringing the plant on stream. Rogers (1983) defines this milestone as the time when the innovation is put into use. This milestone may also assume the form of the 'roll-over' of a new work process or the 'cut-over' to a new system (Rey, 1984). In studying vertical transfers of knowledge, Leonard-Barton defined this milestone as the 'very first use of the technology in a routine production task' (1990a:259). Finally, von Hippel and Tyre (1995) defined this milestone as the commencement of learning-by-doing which, they argued, must be done, and therefore this milestone is likely to be relevant to a broad spectrum of transfers of know-how.

Achievement of satisfactory performance. The fourth milestone is the achievement of a satisfactory level of performance. In Teece's study this milestone occurred when a manufacturing plant reached the expected productivity level, i.e. when the operation was debugged and the plant was running smoothly. Upon reaching this milestone, special provisions made for the ramp-up process are dismantled (Tyre and Hauptman, 1992). Thus, for example, even though productivity may continue to improve, troubleshooters, remaining personnel from the source unit, startup teams, external consultants or subcontractors will most likely quit the recipient unit or change role when this milestone is reached. The criterion for defining satisfactory performance is likely to be industry specific. Thus a steel mini-mill is considered to have achieved a satisfactory level of performance when it reaches break-even. A semiconductor 'fab' is said to achieve this point when it is certified. A bank reaches this point when it can balance its daily operations relying solely on its own back-room personnel.

Each of the four stages – initiation, implementation, ramp-up and integration – can be difficult in their own way. The nature of difficulty at each stage, and possible predictors, are discussed below.

A typology of stickiness

Initiation stickiness

Initiation stickiness is the difficulty in recognizing opportunities to transfer and in acting upon them. An opportunity to transfer exists as soon as the seed for that transfer is formed, i.e. as soon as a gap and knowledge to address the gap are found within the organization. The discovery of a gap may trigger a problemistic search (Cyert and March, 1963) for suitable solutions. Alternatively, slack search may uncover superior practices, thus revealing a previously unsuspected gap or creating a new one (Cyert and March, 1963; Glaser *et al.*, 1983; Rogers, 1983; Zaltman *et al.*, 1973).

The eventfulness of the initiation stage depends on how difficult it is to find an opportunity to transfer and to decide whether or not to pursue it. This becomes more demanding when existing operations are inadequately understood or when relevant and timely measures of performance, as well as internal or external yardsticks, are missing. Furthermore, the opportunity may need further scrutiny in order to understand why or how superior results are obtained by the source. The original rationale for a practice and its nuances are gradually reduced to taken-for-granted beliefs and entrenched habits. Yet, before the transfer can be undertaken, the practice may need to be documented, e.g. by creating process maps or flowcharts, and its rationale reconstructed in order to select what needs to be transferred. Consequently, the initiation of a transfer may require substantial effort to delineate the scope of that transfer, select the timing, assess the costs and establish the mutual obligations of the participants (Ounjian and Carne, 1987:198).

The search for opportunities and the decision to proceed with a transfer inevitably occur under some degree of irreducible uncertainty or causal ambiguity. The source's mastery and ability to articulate a practice is often incomplete, as is the recipient's ability to specify the environment where new knowledge will be applied. Measures of performance used to identify opportunities are often imprecise and subject to fluctuation. It becomes more difficult to assess the real merit of an opportunity and to act upon it. However, this uncertainty is reduced when there is evidence that the knowledge to be transferred has proven robust in other environments and that the source is reputable. When the source is not perceived as reliable, trustworthy or knowledgeable, initiating a transfer from that source will be more difficult, and its advice and example are likely to be challenged and resisted (Walton, 1975).

Implementation stickiness

Following the decision to transfer knowledge, attention shifts to the exchange of information and resources between the source and the recipient. Transfer-specific ties are established between members of the source and the recipient, and information and resource flows will typically increase and possibly peak at this stage. Efforts are made to pre-empt problems through careful planning (Pisano, 1996), especially to avoid the recurrence of problems experienced in previous transfers of the same knowledge, and to help make the introduction of new knowledge less threatening to the recipient (Buttolph, 1992:464; Rice and Rogers, 1980:508–9).

The eventfulness of the implementation stage depends on how challenging it is to bridge the communications gap between the source and the recipient and to fill the recipient's technical gap. Bridging the communications gap may require solving problems caused by incompatibilities of language, coding schemes and cultural conventions. Closing the technical gap may disrupt the normal activities of both source and recipient. It may distract the source from its main mission (unless its mission is to support the transfer) – especially when supporting the transfer means generating additional documents, constructing dedicated equipment, lending or donating its own skilled personnel, or training the recipient's personnel. It may also temporarily disrupt the recipient's operations because existing personnel may have to be retrained or reassigned, new personnel may be hired and trained, infrastructure may have to be modified and upgraded and consultants from the source unit or elsewhere may move temporarily to the recipient. Furthermore, when the recipient unit is large, transfer-related information may not reach all parts of the recipient, thus creating problems of coordination.

Further difficulty may also result from poor coordination between the source and the recipient, especially when the source or the recipient of knowledge deviates from agreed-upon responsibilities. The source or the recipient may do more or less than is expected from them, leading to situations where the recipient usurps roles of the source or where the source intrudes the domain of the recipient (Leonard-Barton, 1990b).

The true motivations of the source and the recipient are likely to be revealed at this stage. The recipient may increase difficulty by ignoring the source's recommendations out of misunderstanding, resentment, or to preserve pride of ownership and status (Rice and Rogers, 1980). The extent of difficulty can be mitigated through planning. However, the extent to which implementation activities can be planned depends on the depth of understanding of the practice, i.e. on causal ambiguity. Oversights during planning can be compensated for through mutual adjustment. The effectiveness of planning, coordination and mutual adjustments are likely to depend on the quality of the relationship between the source and the recipient.

Ramp-up stickiness

Once the recipient begins using acquired knowledge, e.g. starts up a new production facility, rolls over a new process or cuts over to a new system, the main concern becomes identifying and resolving unexpected problems that keep the recipient from matching or exceeding the expectations of post-transfer performance. The ramp-up stage offers a relatively brief window of opportunity to rectify unexpected problems (Tyre and Orlikowski, 1994), where the recipient is likely to begin using new knowledge ineffectively (Adler, 1990; Baloff, 1970; Chew, 1991; Galbraith, 1990), ramping up gradually towards a satisfactory level of performance, often with external assistance.

The eventfulness of the ramp-up phase depends on the number and seriousness of unexpected problems and the effort required to solve them. Unexpected problems may surface because a new environment in which the transferred knowledge is put to use reacts differently than expected, training of personnel turns out to be insufficient or incomplete, trained personnel leave the organization or prove unfit for new roles, or the new practices involve significant changes in the language system and in the shared norms and beliefs underlying the correct interpretation of work directives. Likewise, when the transition to the use of new knowledge is gradual rather than sharp, i.e. when a new practice co-exists over time with the practice it is meant to replace, duplication of effort and resource contention are likely. Unexpected problems become more difficult to resolve the later they occur within the ramp-up stage, because precarious versions of new practices may already have become habitualized and thus more difficult to modify. When new knowledge is put to use in broad scope, i.e. simultaneously rather than sequentially, the scope of incidence of unexpected problems will generally be broader.

Difficulty during the ramp-up stage is thus likely to correspond primarily to the degree of causal ambiguity of the practice. Unexpected problems are easier to resolve when cause–effect relationships for the new practice are understood, and when it is possible to forecast and explain results. The absorptive capacity of the recipient, i.e. the ability to utilize new knowledge, depends on its existing stock of knowledge and skills. Thus the presence of relevant expertise during the ramp-up stage, either from internal or external sources, is crucial to contain costs (Chew, 1991) and delays (Baloff, 1970).

Integration stickiness

Once satisfactory results are initially obtained, the use of the new knowledge gradually becomes routine. This progressive routinization is incipient in every recurring social pattern (Berger and Luckman, 1966). Unless difficulty is encountered in the process, the new practices will blend in the objective, taken-for-granted reality of the organization (Berger and Luckman, 1966; Zucker, 1977). However, when difficulties are encountered, the new practices may be abandoned and, when feasible, revertion to the former status quo may occur.

The eventfulness of the integration phase depends on the effort required to remove obstacles and to deal with challenges to the routinization of the new practice. This involves maintaining a delicate and comprehensive truce in intra-organizational conflict, i.e. a situation where members of the organization are 'content to play their roles…[and where]…manifest conflict follows largely predictable paths and stays within predictable bounds' (Nelson and Winter, 1982:110). This truce may be disturbed by external events such as environmental changes, the arrival of new members or the appearance of a clearly superior alternative (Goodman *et al.*, 1980; Zaltman *et al.*, 1973). Likewise, the truce may be disturbed by internal events such as individual lapses in performance, unmet expectations, unclear rationale for the practice, evidence of dysfunctional consequences of using new knowledge or sudden changes in the scale of activities. Each disturbance to the truce may compound difficulty because each time a contingency is resolved, the terms of the truce become more specific and likely to elicit some resistance.

Organizational sub-units may differ in their ability to maintain routine operation. For example, they may differ in the quality of sensing mechanisms that detect incipient threats to the organizational truce, and they may also differ in their ability to recalibrate situations once the threat is recognized (Goodman and Associates, 1982). The commitment of the recipient to specific practices will become evident during the institutionalization stage, because each time the truce is disturbed the appropriateness of the new practice may be explicitly questioned and re-evaluated, requiring an affirmative 'decision to continue'. This decision may exact a social cost to the recipient (Berger and Luckman, 1966; Goodman and Associates, 1982: 270–1; Nelson and Winter, 1982:112; Tolbert, 1987). For example, preserving the use of new knowledge may require disciplining or removing disruptive individuals who do not accept the new power distribution or other organizational parameters of the new practice.

Note

1. See also Glaser *et al.* (1983): Chapter 7 and Rogers (1983): 164–6.

6

Case Studies

The four types of stickiness – initiation, implementation, ramp-up and integration – are illustrated with findings from in-depth fieldwork in three different settings: Rank Xerox, Banc One and CENTEL, a subsidiary of SPRINT. Initiation stickiness is illustrated with Rank Xerox's difficulties to initiate transfers between its European subsidiaries. Implementation and ramp-up stickiness are illustrated with Banc One's difficulties experienced when converting acquired banks. Integration stickiness is illustrated by CENTEL's difficulties sustaining in each of its divisions a 'best' practice that had already been effectively implemented.[1] Figure 6.1 shows the correspondence between the research sites and the types of stickiness that they help illustrate.

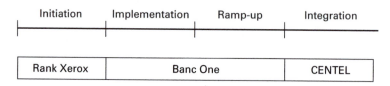

Figure 6.1

Setting

Rank Xerox

Rank Xerox (now Xerox Europe) is a European multinational with operations in all Western European countries, and in Africa and Asia. In 1992, it had 26,000 employees and a turnover of 4 billion ECUs. The early 1990s had been a time of substantial change at both European Rank Xerox and its parent company, Xerox Corporation, headquartered in Stamford, Connecticut. To match the financial performance of the US operation, Managing Director Bernard Fournier launched the Rank Xerox 2000 initiative in September 1992. An important part of the initiative consisted of a reorganization designed to shorten the 'line of sight' between headquarters and customers to match the customer responsiveness levels achieved by the Business Division structure of Xerox US. A main thrust of the RX-2000 initiative was to identify and transfer 'best practices' across countries. Fournier formed a series of expert teams to meet these objectives. The most ambitious initiative, 'Team C', had the goal of increasing incremental revenues by identifying, documenting and transferring best practices associated with discrete sales and marketing processes. While the first wave of this initiative proved successful, the launch of the second wave stalled.

Banc One

From 1982 until 1993, Banc One, a regional retail bank, grew its asset base from $5 billion to over $46 billion mainly by acquiring and affiliating 36 banks.[2] Increasingly larger new affiliates were converted to a standardized product line supported by common data-processing (DP) systems through the 'affiliation' process. An important part of that process was the 'conversion' of the bank to common DP systems and operating procedures. The informal process used to convert early affiliates became progressively formalized. Because brief malfunctions of converted affiliates were prohibitive, achieving flawless implementation of conversions was of utmost importance to Banc One. Indeed, as converted banks grew larger, corporate efforts to make conversions work smoothly took precedence over efforts to develop new products.[3] Yet, to sustain its rapid growth, Banc One strained the scope of its affiliation activities, occasionally encountering limitations in its conversion process, which it then had to adjust. One such occasion, in 1992, was the conversion of Affiliated Bankshares of Colorado, a bank with $2.8 billion in assets. The affiliation of 'Colorado' was announced to the press in November 1991, and the first event related to the conversion process occurred on 21 May 1992 with an overview meeting; the actual conversion process begun in earnest at the conversion kick-off meeting held on 1 October 1992. On 7 May 1993, Colorado closed its doors operating as Affiliated Bankshares and reopened on 10 May as Banc One Colorado, discontinuing at once the reliance on their old systems. That transition is known within Banc One as the 'conversion weekend'. Difficulties experienced prior to conversion weekend illustrate implementation stickiness, while difficulties experienced after the conversion weekend illustrate ramp-up stickiness.

CENTEL

CENTEL was a US provider of local telephone services in six states, and was later acquired by SPRINT. CENTEL awoke late but decisively to simmering competition in local telephone services. To remain viable, it had to learn rapidly how to introduce new services at low costs, which could only be possible if operations were first standardized and then automated. To this end, CENTEL adopted a process-centred quality program to streamline and re-engineer the administrative pieces of five main processes that, taken together, controlled 75–80 per cent of its operations. It cherry picked the best activities from each division to assemble a 'super-process' or best available practice, which was then replicated in all six divisions. In the case of debt collection practices, this fruitful streamlining effort dramatically reduced bad net debt, i.e. the percentage of debt that goes uncollected, from 4 per cent to less than 2 per cent. However, scrutiny of the collection offices a few months after the initial implementation revealed that the degree of persistence of those changes was uneven.

Initiation stickiness at Rank Xerox: Wave II stalls

Best-practices initiatives at Rank Xerox took the form of corporate-level teams. By 1996, Team A had completed the reorganization of Rank Xerox into a matrix of territorial entities coordinated by the European headquarters and global product divisions. The parameters to design the structure and choose the optimal size of the units were based on internal and external productivity benchmarks. The Team A restructuring initiative decreased the 1993 cost base by $240 million. Team B had slashed $50 million by eliminating activities and layers that did not add direct value to the company and to its customers, most notably at Rank Xerox's corporate headquarters in Marlow, UK, where the headcount was reduced by an order of magnitude.

The first wave of the Team C initiative (Wave I) began in 1994. The goal of Wave I was to identify, document and transfer best practices to bring specific products to market to increase revenues. Team C searched for discrete best practices that were contained entirely in a specific location. These best practices would then be transferred to other locations, with the originating unit serving as the working example of that practice, for others units to consult and emulate.

To find those best practices, Team C spent six months searching for best performance in the database and writing to medium-level key executives in each country asking for their best ideas. Of a total of 40 proposed ideas, Team C selected 10 which were then validated *in situ*. The team emerged from this effort with nine validated best practices for revenue growth. The units where best practice was found and validated were designated as benchmarks. Team C then prepared and distributed a set of easy-to-understand books detailing those practices. The nine best practices are detailed below:

MajestiK	An initiative to increase market share in the European colour copier market
Customer Retention	A plan to encourage current customers to repurchase equipment from Rank Xerox by providing special incentives to salespeople for customer retention, as well as technological database aids for tracking customer equipment stocks, usage requirements and contract expiration dates
DocuTech	An initiative to sell offset printers to commercial and educational users by focusing on overall document solutions rather than on traditional product or price selling
New Business Major Accounts	A plan to establish salespeople whose sole responsibility is generating new business
DocuPrint	A plan to accelerate sales of the newly launched line of high-speed network printers, particularly to the banking and insurance industries, by emphasizing the product's image printing capabilities and systems integration features
CSO Competitive MIF Identification	An initiative for the rapid updating of the Rank Xerox company-wide sales database to track competitive information and provide salespeople with reliable leads
Analyst Time Billing	A plan to sell the value-adding, problem-solving consulting services of Rank Xerox technical analysts
XBS	A plan to educate salespeople on how to sell facilities management services effectively through the creation of simple packages and pricing options (i.e. Rank Xerox providing the customer with a packaged service consisting of both equipment and manpower)

Second Hand CEP

An initiative to regain control of the secondhand market for centralized mainframe printers (typically found in data centres) by repurchasing secondhand machines, refurbishing them and reselling them to targeted accounts for which price sensitivity is very high.

The original implementation goals of Wave I were relatively modest: 50 per cent of the opportunities to transfer best practice would be pursued in 75 per cent of the regional units. The corporate office asked each regional unit to choose at least four from the set of nine practices.

Even though overall expectations were met by Wave I, different initiatives had varying degrees of success. Some surpassed expectations, others merely met expectations and some failed to meet expectations.

Team C, Wave I initiative increased revenues by $106 million in the first year, and by $150 million in 1995, at an estimated cost of roughly $1 million per year.

The success of Wave I inspired Team C to set its sights on a more challenging objective for 1995: to define and transfer best practices for salesforce productivity, an overarching core process of the corporation. The projected rewards from this second wave (Wave II) tripled those achieved by Wave I. For Wave II, Team C identified the different components of sales practices in a number of countries and assembled an overall blueprint of all the key sales-related activities, labelled 'Salesforce Management Activity Model', using the best components from each country. A working example of the model did not exist in its totality in any one country, but all of its pieces could be found somewhere within the company.

In concrete terms, implementing the Salesforce Management Activity Model meant standardizing almost every aspect of the salesperson job, which, for most units, meant that their salesforce had to significantly change many of their practices. For example, a traditional belief of the salesforce was that to increase sales one had to spend more time on the road and make more contacts with the customer. However, Team C discovered that, rather than spending more time in the field, the best-performing salespeople spent more time in the office preparing for their field trips, deciding which customers to visit and choosing the optimal timing for the visit, i.e. closest to the moment in which the customer would be making a purchasing decision. Also, unique software had to be developed for each aspect of the sales process and linked to a market database of schedules, performance figures, leads, contacts and other sales information. Salespeople would be able to access the database remotely with their personal computers, and managers would be able to monitor salesperson activity at all times.

Once the documentation for the Salesforce Management Activity Model was completed it was time to put the model into practice. Unlike the case of

Wave I, Team C found that the regional units were much less enthusiastic about this second wave of best practices. The urgency to change had decreased after the resounding success of Wave I led Rank Xerox to out-perform Xerox US in operating benchmarks in 1994 and 1995. Furthermore, because Wave II was based on a laboratory model of the process, Team C could argue but not provide evidence for the usefulness of the process, nor point to a benchmark unit where the process could be observed. Furthermore, the Salesforce Management Activity Model was significantly more complex to grasp than any of Wave I's revenue opportunities because it consisted of several such interdependent modules and required special-ized hardware and software.

Implementation stickiness at Banc One: Colorado doesn't convert

In April 1992, a little over a month after the affiliation, Banc One started the conversion of the 'Colorado' affiliate. The first task was to issue a Conversion Recommendation, which among other things specified that all 42 branches of the six banks composing the Colorado affiliate would be con-verted during the same conversion weekend. Furthermore, it was decided that to accelerate the conversion, the Colorado affiliate would be converted simultaneously to the three systems to which other affiliates had been con-verted only sequentially, letting the converted organizations stabilize before further change was introduced.

The three systems to which Colorado was converted simultaneously were: the Common Systems, comprising software that implemented spe-cific financial products or services; the Branch Automation System, which automated teller and other customer service functions; and the Strategic Banking System, which at the time was a major competitive weapon for Banc One because it integrated all account information pertaining to a spe-cific customer allowing bank officers to uncover and offer customized solu-tions to customers' needs from 'cradle to grave'.

Besides the fact that all banks would be converted simultaneously and to a set of three systems, other aspects of the Colorado conversion made it even more complex and risky. The conversion manager, Barry Jones, was concerned that a new data-processing centre in Phoenix, Arizona, the Central Processing Unit for the bank operations, had to be set up and tested during the conversion to serve the Banc One banks in the state of Colorado. He was also concerned that required regulatory approvals were still pending without a clear resolution date in sight. Barry wondered how much more could be 'squeezed' into the conversion schedule.

The Colorado conversion limped along to the conversion weekend. The Colorado affiliate seemed motivated by the prospects of matching the much admired Banc One's operational excellence but it became increasingly apparent that it had only partial understanding of Banc One's systems and operating procedures. F' .' example, Colorado banks insisted in devising their own set of forms Fy modifying existing ones, rather than adapting Banc One forms which were more closely aligned to the new systems. Another early sign occurred during the last 30 days before conversion weekend, when Colorado personnel scrambled to prepare detailed operating procedures for their banks. As described by an experienced observer: 'They went into a panic. They started shooting from the hip. They would write a procedure and send it to the branches and not all branches will get it.' As a branch manager described the situation: 'I've got a stack of procedures from operations this thick one week. How do they expect me to read it?'

Difficulties developed also in the case of training. Colorado insisted in taking responsibility and control for their own training, but, again, without internal education infrastructure and without internal training centres. Banc One did not have sufficient professional trainers to deliver the required training to Colorado's 2100 strong staff. So they needed to set up at least 12 training centres, and to train trainers selected from among Colorado personnel, who had their own ideas about the appropriate training needs.

Ramp-up stickiness at Banc One: teething problems of a converted Colorado

Monday 10 May, the first day that Colorado operated with Banc One systems, was the busiest day the bank had ever had. At 10.30 in the morning, Branch Automation (BA) System went down because it could not keep up with the volume of transactions. The help-desk problem report read 'Branch Automation: Volumes greater than expected, Response time unacceptable (7 min), and System down for most of the day'.[4] The crash was of such severity that two months later the system continued to crash. During that first day, several problems were reported for Strategic Banking System (SBS) and for Common Systems. In total, 27 problems were reported on the first day. Figure 6.2 shows the number of problems experienced for each day of the first week.

The second day things did not start well because some of the SBS problems continued. Besides the major application problems there were also minor errors as a result of oversights during testing. After the first week, most of the major application processing problems (the application cannot start or end successfully) were resolved. The second week was dominated by major problems with Branch Automation. Figure 6.3 depicts the system reject rate for the second, third and fourth weeks of operations.

The number of rejects created by the BA system generated a lot of back-room exceptions. The back-room people from Colorado did not know how to deal with these because their training and some of the operating procedures

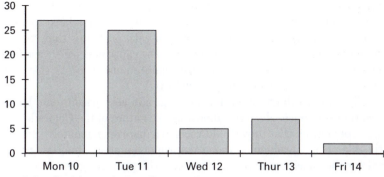

Figure 6.2 *Problems during first week*

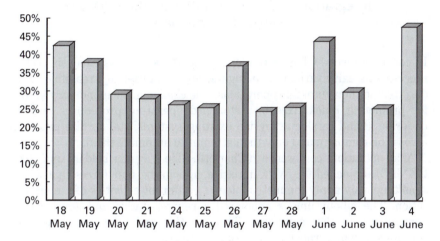

Figure 6.3 *System reject rate*

of their own making were deficient. This reflected immediately in demands for support from all levels of the support network.

An elaborate three-layer support network was put in place to support the ramp-up of Colorado. In addition to the service centre, support specialists were available on-site in several locations, and a hot-line was established which linked to an elaborate communication tree with beepers, cell phones and electronic mail.

During the first week of operations, the entire support network, including the 'experts' of level 3, was kept on its toes. Even the elaborate support infrastructure turned out to be insufficient to cope with the unusual demands of the first two weeks of operations. Thirty out of the 42 geographically dispersed branches had to receive on-site support. Unprecedented hardware and software problems were occurring in some of the unusually large branches. Some of the problems were created not by a particular system but by the interaction between the systems. The mostly specialized staff at Client Services could competently answer questions about their specific operations but were unable to deal with problems that required a systemic solution. Efforts to analyse *in situ* the cause of rejects were initially hampered by the BA system's cryptic maintenance reports that did not specify why transactions were being rejected.

Finally, the coordination within the Colorado conversion team lapsed at critical times because, given the almost heroic nature of the Colorado conversion, people feared that they would receive a disproportionately large share of the blame for problems, and a disproportionately small share of the credit for the sacrifices necessary to make the project work.

Integration stickiness at CENTEL: the SHOULD scenario does not persist

In concrete terms, CENTEL adopted the Work Process Analysis (WPA) process – an early variant of re-engineering – in order to streamline, standardize and then automate operations. The challenge, in an industry known for promoting quick fixes into standard operating procedures, was to understand and catalogue myriad existing systems, standardize practices across the company, and only then attempt to automate them.

At an operations conference in Charlottesville, Virginia, held in April 1991, CENTEL launched the WPA initiative, appointing four forces that would simultaneously apply the methodology to different activities of the organization. The labour unions appointed a representative and approved all nominations to the task force. Through this and other measures, the process was made transparent to the workforce.

As shown in Figure 6.4, the WPA process consists of three phases – IS, SHOULD and COULD – each resulting in a major 'scenario'.

During the IS phase, information is gathered to document current operations, to find out how things are actually done. The IS phase culminates with the IS scenario. The taskforce then designs a standard process for each individual activity that will be implemented in all units, taking into consideration state-specific regulations and possible retraining costs. This is the SHOULD scenario. The COULD scenario yields the best possible design for all operational activities in a world without constraints.

The collections taskforce, led by Joan Campbell, was charged with analysing the activities of the collections departments, responsible for collecting overdue payments. These departments relied mostly on manually dialled phone calls and personal visits. Dramatic improvement could be achieved by automating these operations, using, for example, an automatic dialler to initiate calls so that employees could spend time on other productive pursuits.

The collections taskforce dashed past the other taskforces through the milestones of the WPA process. The implementation progressed swiftly

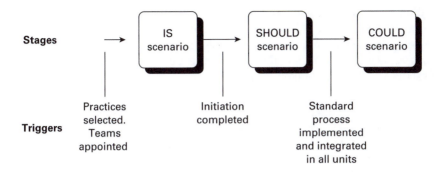

Figure 6.4 *The WPA process*

because it had to meet contractual deadlines to install the automatic diallers and also because there was a simple, straightforward performance benchmark – the percentage of bad net debt (bills remaining uncollected). AT&T, their major client, would immediately reward improvements in bad net debt. From the beginning, the progress of the collections taskforce was CENTEL's most tangible indicator of the overall effect of the WPA initiative on the day-to-day operations of the company.

Difficulties started midway through the SHOULD phase. Developing a standard process that would optimize everyone's performance was more difficult than they had anticipated. An important hurdle was inter-office rivalry. Each office argued and tried to prove that the processes in their state should be designated as the benchmark, even though many knew that other offices actually outperformed them. For this reason, disagreement continued to prevail over the contents of the standard maps. Each state had different reasons for disagreeing with the official benchmarks, and resolution of disparities was laborious and time-consuming. By mid-May the SHOULD scenario had been validated to be about 85 per cent complete.

Upon close scrutiny, the collection taskforce discovered that the integration of the SHOULD scenario was delayed because, briefly after the initial implementation, offices began to introduce changes to the agreed SHOULD plans. They found it difficult to monitor the persistence of changes in remote offices with few employees. Furthermore, less importance was ascribed to a full completion of the SHOULD because corporate management announced preliminary plans for the COULD stage, without waiting for the full completion of the SHOULD scenario. When enquiring about discrepancies, the collections team discovered that many of the offices that had initially implemented the SHOULD scenario abandoned those changes later and returned to their prior practices. CENTEL's senior management appointed two consultants from the CENTEL Quality Institute to research why associates failed to comply with standard procedures. With evidence gathered from employee interviews, focus groups and team observations, they concluded that deficient systems support, associates attitudes and beliefs about the future, and mere excuses (it just won't work) accounted for that reality. As CENTEL discovered, the persistence of the SHOULD practices could not be taken for granted.

Summary

Team C's Wave II illustrates how initiation stickiness was experienced by Rank Xerox. The recipients were sceptical of a complex process for which no evidence of usefulness could be marshalled and for which there was no working example or benchmark unit. Furthermore, there was less urgency to improve and change. The operational difficulties experienced initially by those most involved in the process escalated to a point where they required the intervention of Fournier.

Likewise, at the height of the Colorado conversion crisis, there were daily phone calls between the then CEO of Banc One and the CEO of the Colorado affiliate. The difficulties that led to those phone calls provide a dramatic illustration of implementation stickiness and of ramp-up stickiness. The problems of implementation stemmed from an unusually large conversion effort that exceeded Banc One's capability to train and the ability of Colorado's willingness and ability to absorb new practices. The unexpected problems experienced during ramp-up were mostly a result of the unpreparedness of the recipient as well as the poorly understood interactions between the three systems.

In the case of CENTEL, while their senior management was initially involved throughout the WPA process, they progressively delegated responsibility to the Team Leaders as the implementation showed signs of relatively uneventful progress. When it became evident that some offices were backsliding to prior practices, senior management became intensely interested in the reasons that were preventing the integration. With the help of the two consultants, they found out that those difficulties were created by unmotivated associates who for a long time had grown accustomed to a specific way of doing things and were reluctant to abandon them, even with evidence that there were better ways of doing things. Inter-office rivalries exacerbated those problems.

The impossibility to initiate Wave II, the dramatic consequences of Colorado's implementation and ramp-up problems, and the lack of persistence of CENTEL practices were problems that exceed the base rate of eventfulness of a typical transfer, were widely noticed within the organization and required a particularly intense effort to be solved.

Actors whose attention would not have been normally required – Bernard Fournier, the Rank Xerox Managing Director, John McCoy, the Banc One's CEO and Paul Wilson, CENTEL's Vice-President for customer services – got involved on an exceptional basis to expedite the identification of possible solutions and to enable and coordinate their implementation.

Besides providing a vivid illustration of the reality of stickiness at each stage of the process, when taken together the three cases suggest that different factors lay at the root of the difficulties experienced at different stages of the process. This, in turn, suggests two questions: which barriers are the best predictors of difficulty at each stage of the transfer and which barriers are the best predictors overall?

I explore these two questions in the next chapter.

Notes

1. The interested reader should refer to Appendix 1 on technical research methods for a description of this phase of the research.

2. Banc One Corporation, *1991 Annual Report*. See chart on p. 10.

3. See Uyterhoeven, 1994:17.

4. Banc One Colorado Conversion Processing Problems, week 1 as of 14 May 1993.

Statistical Findings

This chapter presents the results of statistical analysis aimed at identifying which were the best predictors of difficulty for each stage of the transfer and, overall, for the transfers of this study. The findings stem from the analysis of data collected through a two-step questionnaire survey.

Data and analysis

The findings stem from a statistical analysis of data collected from 122 transfers of 38 practices in 8 companies: AMP, AT&T Paradyne, British Petroleum, Burmah Castrol, Chevron Corporation, EDS, Kaiser Permanente and Rank Xerox. The sample contains both technical practices – e.g. software development procedures and drawing standards – and administrative practices – e.g. upward appraisal and activity-based costing (ABC). See Appendix 3 for a fuller list of the practices studied.

These data were gathered in two steps. In the first step, a preliminary 'test' was administered to over sixty companies that expressed initial interest in participating in the study. The test was designed to establish whether the companies would be able to identify specific transfer attempts, would be willing and able to provide adequate information about those attempts and would identify knowledgeable individuals to complete the questionnaires. Only twelve completed this first phase of the survey and eight were invited to participate in the second phase.

The second step of the survey was devised to assess the importance of the predictors of difficulty. To obtain a balanced perspective on each transfer, one questionnaire was sent to the source, one to the recipient and one to a third party to the transfer. The final sample consisted of 271 usable questionnaires, making for a response rate of 61 per cent. In terms of the type of respondent, 110 questionnaires were received from sources units, 101 from recipient units and 60 from third parties. Average item non-response was lower than 5 per cent. On average 7.3 questionnaires were received for each practice studied.

Companies were instructed to rule out practices that could be performed by a single individual and to choose practices that required the coordinated effort of many. With this criterion in mind, they were asked to search for inter-unit transfers of major activities or processes, and to prefer transfers that proved difficult to implement and in which the recipient found it challenging to match the outcomes obtained by the source.

Multiple regression analysis was used to assess the importance of predictors at each stage of the transfer and canonical correlation analysis was used to assess the overall importance of each predictor. A complete account of the methodology used is provided in Appendix 1.

Predictors of difficulty for each stage of the transfer

The importance of each predictor is assessed by running separate regressions for each one of the four types of stickiness: initiation stickiness, implementation stickiness, ramp-up stickiness and integration stickiness. Table 7.1 displays the findings from the four regressions.

Several conclusions can be drawn from the findings. First, the pattern of results is consistent with the general expectation that barriers matter

Table 7.1   *Predictors of stickiness for each stage of the transfer*

| | Standardized beta coefficients (t – value) | | | |
| | Stickiness Initiating | Stickiness Implementing | Stickiness Ramp-up | Stickiness Integrating |
Variable	(I)	(II)	(III)	(IV)
Causal ambiguity	0.20**	0.23**	0.24**	0.16*
	(2.74)	(3.32)	(3.39)	(2.50)
Unproven knowledge	0.27**	0.11+	−0.09	−0.09
	(3.89)	(1.72)	(−1.23)	(−1.43)
Source lacks motivation	0.07	0.17*	0.16*	0.06
	(0.92)	(2.33)	(2.21)	(0.97)
Source not perceived as reliable	0.27**	0.17*	0.24**	−0.05
	(3.59)	(2.25)	(3.23)	(−0.76)
Recipient lacks motivation	0.10	−0.07	−0.14*	0.19**
	(1.35)	(−0.95)	(−2.05)	(3.07)
Recipient lacks absorptive capacity	0.11	0.47**	0.49**	0.45**
	(1.37)	(5.87)	(6.08)	(6.07)
Recipient lacks retentive capacity	−0.01	−0.03	−0.43**	0.01
	(−0.10)	(−0.46)	(−5.73)	(0.20)
Barren organizational context	−0.04	−0.06	0.21**	0.21**
	(−0.55)	(−0.81)	(2.86)	(3.18)
Ardous relationship	0.05	0.16*	0.07	0.19**
	(0.70)	(2.38)	(1.12)	(3.17)
Spontaneity	−0.16*	−0.10+	0.00	0.00
	(−2.53)	(−1.71)	(0.06)	(0.03)
Adj.-R²	**0.42**	**0.51**	**0.52**	**0.64**
N	166	150	158	142

+$p<.10$ *$p<.05$ **$p<.01$

differently at different stages of the transfer. In particular, factors affecting the opportunity to transfer, such as a proven practice or a reliable source, are more likely to predict difficulty during the initiation phase, whereas factors affecting the execution of the transfer, such as the degree of motivation of the recipient or its absorptive capacity, are more likely to predict difficulty during the implementation phases.

Furthermore, some predictors stand out because they are important in at least three of the four phases of the transfer. Causal ambiguity predicts difficulty at all four stages of the transfer. Its effects remain large and significant throughout. Absorptive capacity matters for all three stages of the implementation. For those three stages, the effect is large and significant. Absorptive capacity, however, does not seem to be significant during the initiation phase. Finally, the perceived reliability of the source, whether the source is perceived as both able and well intended, matters during the first three phases of the transfer. Perceived reliability matters particularly during the initiation and the ramp-up phases, which is when the example of the source often plays a crucial role as either an element of persuasion or as a reference to solve problems that arise with the replica.

Finally, two unexpected findings are particularly intriguing. One of them is the counter-intuitive finding that a motivated recipient can intensify, rather than mitigate, the difficulty encountered during the ramp-up stage (see Table 7.1, Stickiness Ramp-up (III) column). This finding is consistent with studies of the diffusion of innovations where highly motivated adopters have been found to exacerbate problems of implementation by prematurely dismissing outside help, expanding seemingly straightforward modifications into major projects, making unnecessary modifications to preserve pride of ownership and status or to let out hidden resentment (Rice and Rogers, 1980; Tyre and Orlikowski, 1994) or switching to new practices at a sub-optimal moment because of unchecked enthusiasm (Baloff, 1970). This counter-intuitive finding suggests the intriguing hypothesis that a highly motivated recipient can be a double-edged sword, in that it may help initiate a transfer but it might also complicate its implementation.

The other stable but unexpected result is the negative coefficient on the lack of retentive capacity during ramp-up (see Table 7.1, Stickiness Ramp-up (III) column). This construct, which was expected to be significant during the integration stage, turned out to be significant only during the ramp-up stage and with opposite sign. This finding may therefore be an indication of the presence of unlearning barriers (Szulanski, 1996).

Because questionnaires were administered shortly after practices had been implemented by the recipient, those practices were unlikely to have been fully institutionalized by the time measurement occurred (Lawless, 1987; Tyre and Orlikowski, 1994). Thus, to the extent that this construct measures the degree of institutionalization of a practice, a high score of institutionalization early in the integration stage must represent institutionalization of *pre-existing* practices. The more institutionalized a pre-existing practice is, the higher the effort required to dismantle it, i.e. the higher the unlearning barrier (Hedberg, 1981; see also Hamel, 1991).

Predictors of difficulty, overall

The overall importance of each predictor was assessed with a canonical correlation analysis. This kind of analysis is used to assess relationships between two sets of variables. The predictors constitute one set; indicators of the different types of stickiness constitute the other. The results of the analysis are as follows:

$$
\begin{aligned}
&\begin{aligned}
&+ 0.15 * \text{Stickiness Outcome} \\
&+ 0.31 * \text{Stickiness Initiating} \\
&+ 0.30 * \text{Stickiness Implementing} \\
&+ 0.07 * \text{Stickiness Ramp-up} \\
&+ 0.44 * \text{Stickiness Integrating}
\end{aligned}
\ = \
\begin{aligned}
&+ 0.34 * \text{Knowledge Causal Ambiguity} \\
&+ 0.09 * \text{Knowledge Unprovenness} \\
&+ 0.05 * \text{Source Lacks Motivation} \\
&+ 0.09 * \text{Source Lacks Perceived Reliability} \\
&+ 0.18 * \text{Recipient Lacks Motivation} \\
&+ 0.53 * \text{Recipient Lacks Absorptive Capacity} \\
&- 0.25 * \text{Recipient Lacks Retentive Capacity} \\
&+ 0.10 * \text{Context Barren} \\
&+ 0.33 * \text{Relationship Arduous}
\end{aligned}
\end{aligned}
$$

The first question one needs to ask is how strong is the overall relationship between the two groups of variables. Canonical analysis yields a score called canonical-R, which can be interpreted as the simple correlation between the weighted sums of scores from each set of variables. This score is fairly substantial (.87) and highly significant ($p < .001$), suggesting that the two groups of variables share about 75 per cent of the variance. Additional analysis detailed in Appendix 1 allows us to establish that, given the value of the predictors, it is possible to account for roughly 45 per cent of the variance on the stickiness variables.

The relative importance of each predictor is given by its coefficient in Table 7.1. The larger the absolute value of a coefficient, the more important it is the predictor. The results suggest that the three most important barriers are the lack of absorptive capacity of the recipient (.54), causal ambiguity (.34) and an arduous relationship between the source and the recipient (.33).

Like in the analysis of the importance of the predictors at different stages of the transfer, the coefficient for the recipient's lack of retentive capacity emerges unexpectedly with a large and negative coefficient (−.25). As discussed in the previous section, a potential explanation for this finding is that retentive capacity, when measured early in the integration stage, represents to some extent the formalized routine use of *previous* practices. Hence, unlearning (Hedberg, 1981) will be required to replace prior knowledge (Hamel, 1991). Dismantling retentive capacity for prior knowledge contributes to stickiness.

Summary

This chapter has identified the best predictors of difficulty for each stage of the transfer process and also the best predictors of difficulty overall for the transfers of this study. The findings stem from a statistical analysis of data collected from 122 transfers of 38 practices in 8 companies: AMP, AT&T Paradyne, British Petroleum, Burmah Castrol, Chevron Corporation, EDS, Kaiser Permanente and Rank Xerox.

Several conclusions are drawn from the findings. First, the pattern of results is consistent with the general expectation that barriers matter differently at different stages of the transfer. Furthermore, causal ambiguity, absorptive capacity and perceived reliability stand out because they have large and significant coefficients in at least three of the four phases of the transfer. Finally, two counter-intuitive findings suggest that unlearning barriers may be at work, and also the intriguing hypothesis that a highly motivated recipient can be a double-edged sword in that it may help initiate a transfer but it might also complicate its implementation.

The analysis of the overall importance of the different predictors reveals that the three most important barriers are the lack of absorptive capacity of the recipient, causal ambiguity and an arduous relationship between the source and the recipient.

The next chapter discusses the implications of these findings for research and for practice.

8

Research and Practical Implications

This chapter suggests some implications of this study for further research on stickiness and for the practice of knowledge transfer. In relation to extant research on stickiness, this study integrates recent conceptual insights into the characteristics of knowledge with elements of the social context, elements which were for the most part neglected in prior studies. Accordingly, a distinction is made between the characteristics of the knowledge transferred and the characteristics of the situation in which the transfer occurs. This study offers also a typology as well as alternative ways to measure stickiness.

The discussion of implications for research ends with suggestions for more specialized research on stickiness and on its antecedents. One type of specialized enquiry focuses on deepening our understanding of the effect of specific factors, such as causal ambiguity or absorptive capacity. Besides considering the isolated effect of these factors, interesting questions arise when one considers their interaction. The example of the interaction between the source's perceived trustworthiness and causal ambiguity is elaborated in some detail. The discussion of implications for research concludes with a brief remark about the promise of a pragmatic perspective on knowledge transfer for the study of stickiness and of its consequences.

The development of implications for practice begins with the identification of three different kinds of transfer problems, which is used as a point of departure to speculate about possible actions that could be taken to facilitate each stage of the transfer. Next, practical questions that typically arise during the initiation of knowledge transfers are explored empirically using data collected in this study. These include the question of who should be the first recipient of an internal best-practice transfer, when there are several viable candidates to choose from, and also the question of how senior management interventions could affect stickiness.

Implications for research

This study and stickiness research

Knowledge transfer occurs in a number of different situations. Such situations could be roughly classified into two broad categories. One category consists of the so-called 'vertical' transfers of knowledge, which typically occur between differentiated, specialized groups. A typical vertical transfer takes place between research and design activities, design and manufacturing activities, or customers and users. For this kind of transfers, the main challenge consists of transforming the contents of knowledge across functional boundaries (see Hoopes and Postrel, 1999, for the characterization of how problems may unfold; and Carlile, 2002, for a recent review).

The second category is that of spatial replication (O'Dell and Jackson Grayson, 1998; Winter and Szulanski, 2001). The main challenge in this category consists of the need to re-create practices effectively in different geographical locales. Unlike in vertical transfers, this second category of transfers occurs mostly among similar entities. Occasionally, a third party such as a corporate function or a consultant may act as the source of the practice and attempt to disseminate it to other organizational sub-units. Although this situation has the semblance of a 'vertical' transfer, such a third party would probably be acting as an intermediating agent between the original source and the recipient.

Two notions of stickiness have emerged from the study of knowledge transfers. Von Hippel's (1994) seminal treatment of stickiness as the cost of transferring a given unit of information in a form usable by the recipient has as backdrop transfers of knowledge between users and developers of technological innovations – transfers that are considered to be vertical in nature. Von Hippel concentrates on the consequences of stickiness to explain the resulting spatial configuration of problem-solving activities. Because he is mostly interested in the consequences of stickiness, rather than on explaining stickiness *per se*, von Hippel is inclusive with respect to cause, citing attributes of the information, and characteristics and decisions of the donor and the recipient as possible causes of stickiness. So far empirical studies in this stream have inferred stickiness mostly from attributes of the information transferred, such as newness (Ogawa, 1998) or tacitness (Zander, 1991).

In contrast, Teece's (1976) study of the cost of international transfers of technology emerged from a backdrop of spatial replication, i.e. the second category of transfers. Teece studied 26 projects of international technology transfer within multinational corporations. He focused on the cost of transfer, which, he argued, is to some degree an indication of the ease or difficulty of transfer. Characteristics of both the technology and of the recipient unit feature prominently among the factors that he considered to explain the cost of transfer.

This study belongs in the second category. Even though it draws also on lessons learned from the study of vertical transfers of knowledge, the underlying conception of transfer assumes the existence of a working example or template of the knowledge to be transferred. A special effort is made to provide a comprehensive and systematic treatment of factors that may predict stickiness.

A *comprehensive typology of predictors of stickiness*

Most contemporary studies of stickiness and knowledge transfer are premised on the observation that knowledge is 'something more' or even 'something else' than fully codified information. The object of transfer, the target information or practice may have tacit elements (Kogut and Zander, 1992; Nonaka 1994; Polanyi 1962) that are difficult to grasp or articulate. Such characteristics may affect many transfer activities. Accordingly, characteristics of knowledge are an essential component of the typology of predictors of stickiness.

The other elements of this typology are derived using Shannon's SRMC, i.e. source, recipient, message and channel (Rogers, 1994) as organizing metaphor. Shannon's model, developed from a broad survey of transfer situations, provides a parsimonious yet comprehensive organizing framework that is implicitly, if not explicitly, relied upon in most studies of knowledge transfer.

Thus, the typology of predictors of stickiness advanced in this study considers, in addition to characteristics of knowledge, also characteristics of the source of knowledge, of the recipient of knowledge and of the 'channel', i.e. the relationship between source and the recipient and of the social context in which the transfer does (or does not) occur.

The *distinction between attributes of the knowledge and those of the situation*

It is sometimes useful to distinguish between the characteristics of the knowledge transferred and those of the situation in which it is transferred. Such distinction reflects an important underlying feature of this study: stickiness is seen to be an attribute of the transfer, not of the knowledge transferred. Stickiness can be affected by attributes of both the knowledge transferred and of the situation in which the transfer occurs. Each one of these dimensions may vary quite significantly independently of one another.

The idea that stickiness is a characteristic of the transfer, not just of the knowledge transferred, is consistent with von Hippel's notion of stickiness, because in his calculation of the cost of transferring a given unit of information he includes the cost of bringing the information to a form in which it is usable by the recipient. Such a component of the cost is most likely to depend on the situation in which a transfer occurs.

The principal implication of viewing stickiness as a property of the transfer, and not the knowledge transferred, is that the transfer of the same unit of knowledge may be sticky in one situation and non-sticky in another. Thus, for example, a unit of information may be transferable at low cost in one situation and at a considerably higher cost in another. More generally, stickiness depends not only on the characteristics of the knowledge transferred but also on those of the situation in which it is being transferred.

Barriers to transfer and generative mechanisms for stickiness

The typology of barriers is constructed by departing from the observation of the distinctiveness of knowledge assets and using Shannon's metaphor to complete the specification. The way in which each barrier affects stickiness is specified to varying degrees of depth, drawing on extant, and rather idiosyncratic, literature.

The next step in developing our understanding of stickiness consists, therefore, of searching for generative mechanisms that will provide a more parsimonious and integrative understanding of how barriers affect stickiness. Such mechanisms must provide the basis for models that generate a pattern of implications that matches the sum total of those barrier-specific explanations.

Two such logics could provide a starting point. One suggests that barriers, regardless of their exact nature, increase stickiness by preventing the initiation of a transfer, i.e. by decreasing the probability that a transfer would be undertaken. Such would be the case, for example, of a factor that increases dramatically the perceived cost of a transfer. The other logic suggests that barriers, regardless of their exact nature, increase stickiness by precipitating the moment in which the recipient ceases to refer to the source's knowledge or the working example, and continues to implement the transfer on its own. While such referencing is likely to cease anyway, premature abandonment of existing knowledge might increase stickiness.

Causal ambiguity as the central attribute of knowledge

When transfer of knowledge is seen as a quest to reproduce results obtained elsewhere, it then becomes evident that causal ambiguity affects such transfers of knowledge in a fundamental way. That is because the advice of the source could significantly facilitate the reproduction of results by, for example, pre-empting costly rediscovery of information that exists already.

The potential contribution of the source, however, is limited by the degree of irreducible uncertainty in the understanding of why the exemplar works. The existence of causal ambiguity means that the precise reasons for success or failure cannot be determined, even ex-post, and that it is therefore impossible to produce a unique list of the key components of that knowledge and of how they interact.

Thus, causal ambiguity might limit the depth of understanding of the source, because in such circumstances there is often a gap between the formal description – as represented in training programmes and manuals – and actual work practices. The higher the causal ambiguity, the wider the gap between description and reality. This limits the depth of the source's understanding of the functioning of what has to be copied.

When there is no gap, i.e. without causal ambiguity, the description of practice is likely to correspond closely, if not exactly, to reality. The problem of transfer in this case becomes the problem of accurately communicating relevant information, because this allows the recipient to reconstruct every relevant detail of the activities.

However, when the functioning of the exemplar is not completely understood, multiple explanations may co-exist, because it is not possible to choose one and rule out the others based on available evidence. When this is the case, the cost and the degree of difficulty are likely to increase. The 'transfer' could turn into a protracted iterative process where initially unsatisfactory results are successively improved through repeated comparisons with the exemplar.

Causal ambiguity thus becomes a fundamental attribute of knowledge when the purpose is to understand difficulty. When there is causal ambiguity, one must explicitly consider the possibility that the exemplar is only partially understood by the source. Such transfers are qualitatively different, making causal ambiguity a fundamental source of difficulty to knowledge transfer. Perhaps more than anything else, understanding that knowledge is something more or something else than codified information entails accepting the possibility that everything is not well known at the source, and carefully considering the consequences.

Opening up the black-box of transfer – the four stages, four types of stickiness

If the transfer could turn into an iterative process of non-negligible duration, then another avenue towards advancing our understanding of stickiness consists of opening up the black-box of transfer in order to understand the process of transfer. Such an effort to unveil the mechanics of knowledge transfer, which seems hardly necessary when one conceives of transfers as almost instantaneous events, becomes justified and potentially fruitful when transfers may turn into protracted iterative processes. Understanding how transfers happen could help unveil how difficulties are created, how different sources contribute to them and what can be done to overcome them.

This study could therefore be seen as a first step in opening up the black-box of transfer by taking a diachronic[1] approach to the analysis of the transfer process. The process model proposed and illustrated in this book provides, hopefully, a constructive way to incorporate difficulty into the analysis of knowledge transfer. By distinguishing between initiation stickiness, implementation stickiness, ramp-up stickiness and integration stickiness, the model provides one possible way to describe and to examine empirically the evolution of difficulty more precisely.

Potential avenues for future research

Improving our understanding of stickiness entails understanding how stickiness comes about, understanding the factors that cause stickiness, and identifying meaningful and significant interactions between those factors. To the extent that this study is a worthy point of departure for further study of stickiness, this suggests three broad directions for future research to further our understanding of stickiness: studying specific stages of the transfer process closely; isolating the effect of specific factors; and identifying meaningful and significant interactions.

Focusing on a specific stage

Trading breath for depth could be a particularly fruitful approach to understand difficulty in the process of transfer, as different actions may be appropriate for different stages of the transfer. By exploring the effect of different barriers separately at each stage of the transfer process, it was found in this study that, contrary to expectations, a motivated recipient could create unnecessary difficulty during the ramp-up stage by doing too much too early, even though, as expected, a motivated recipient was found to reduce difficulty during the early steps of implementation. A focused investigation of the activities of the recipient at the ramp-up stage may help unravel this unexpected effect of recipient's motivation. Thus, for example, Terwiesch and Bohn (2001) focus on the ramp-up stage and find that there is a trade-off between learning and production. Early learning is more valuable but could have a high opportunity cost. Such trade-offs may affect ramp-up stickiness.

Focusing on the effects of a specific barrier

Recent conceptual advantages have afforded researchers a new view on knowledge transfer barriers. In particular, two types of barriers are now better understood: knowledge-related barriers such as absorptive capacity or causal ambiguity, and elements of the social context such as the strength of the social tie between source and recipient. Researchers have begun to study closely the effects of specific barriers for intra- and inter-firm knowledge transfer.

Identifying significant and meaningful interactions between barriers

Besides their direct effects on stickiness, barriers may interact to produce non-obvious second-order results. We have identified causal ambiguity as a fundamental barrier because it affects qualitatively the nature of a transfer. Thus, causal ambiguity seems to be a natural choice to begin the quest to identify meaningful interactions.

Thus, for example, while the perceived trustworthiness of the source has beneficial effects on the effectiveness of knowledge transfer that have long been known to exist, it can also promote dysfunctional behaviours to which attention has only recently been directed.

Indeed, causal ambiguity may moderate the total effect of trustworthiness. Trustworthiness may simultaneously promote both functional and dysfunctional behaviours. On the one hand, it may foster receptivity; on the other, it may lessen the perceived need and the incentives for vigilance. Which facet of this intricate effect is dominant is likely to depend on the level of causal ambiguity.

When causal ambiguity is low, trustworthiness contributes to the effectiveness of the transfer because a suitably motivated source can be trusted to supply advice for which additional validation is seldom necessary. Thus, receptivity translates into greater accuracy and vigilance is likely to prove redundant.

However, when causal ambiguity is high, trustworthiness may prove counter-productive. As argued earlier, causal ambiguity limits the potential contribution of the source. Yet, because the source is perceived to be trustworthy the recipient may delay or inhibit efforts to validate and to supplement the source's advice while change is still possible. Under these conditions, receptivity may be less critical than vigilance. Trustworthiness may increase the incidence of difficulty.

To conclude, it may be worthwhile to reconsider the fundamental premises that guide our approach to the study of stickiness. Indeed, the logic of barriers, which is based on the signalling metaphor, implies that stickiness occurs in exceptional circumstances, i.e. when barriers are encountered, and that normality is restored by removing those barriers. Such logic is at odds with the observation that stickiness is pervasive, that stickiness is the norm rather than the exception.

It is for this reason that perhaps another potentially fruitful avenue for stickiness research consists of exploring alternative theoretical perspectives that recognize the difficulty inherent in social action. Such perspectives would naturally imply a more pervasive incidence of stickiness, i.e. that stickiness is a an integral part of the process of knowledge transfer.

One such perspective is the so-called pragmatic view of knowledge (see Carlile, 2002, for a review). Such a perspective sees transfers in terms of the practical and political problems that they pose to social agents. The pragmatist scholar starts from the presumption that social action requires effort. Difficulty, if such an approach is taken, is no longer an anomaly; rather it is normalcy. It is expected that knowledge transfers require effort. When that is the case, then the challenge of studying stickiness becomes the challenge of identifying the kinds of problems that surface, the nature of the effort that has to be exerted to resolve them, and the expected and unexpected consequences that resolving one kind of problem may have on creating or resolving others.

Thus, a pragmatic perspective evokes a different view of transfers. Transfers of knowledge involve unending problem solving. For the pragmatists, problems are not just different in degree but also different in kind. Such a line of thinking suggests that the emphasis of the research community could be profitably re-directed to articulate carefully a typology of problems that would define stickiness, a task for which hopefully this study provides a useful starting point.

Implications for practice

Different stages, different actions

It is almost a truism that the timing of managerial action could significantly affect the outcome. This is why having a map of the process of transfer could help managers in refining the timing of interventions aimed at facilitating knowledge transfers.

The process model provides a rather general, yet nuanced, description of how a transfer happens by specifying important milestones and the activities between these milestones. The process model is also the starting point for suggesting four classes of problems that could be confronted during a transfer: problems of initiation, implementation, ramping up and integration.

Such distinctions suggest how the process model can be used to calibrate expectations about the kind of problems that might be encountered at each phase of the transfer. By identifying the stage of the transfer where difficulties are encountered or expected, one could infer the incidence of specific barriers.

Conversely, when evaluating the main origins of difficulty in a particular transfer situation, Table 7.1 (page 53) could be used to identify those stages of the process which are likely to demand comparatively more managerial attention, i.e. where more difficulties are to be expected given the origins of difficulty identified as important. For example, if the source unit does not appear sufficiently motivated to support the transfer, difficulties are to be expected, in particular, when the recipient attempts to ramp up to the expected level of performance. Likewise if the recipient is not motivated to support the transfer, the highest level of difficulty is going to be experienced during the integration of the new practice into the recipient's operations.

Issues when initiating a transfer

Who goes first?

When many potential recipients exist for a staggered transfer, the designer of that transfer is likely to be confronted with the need to choose from the

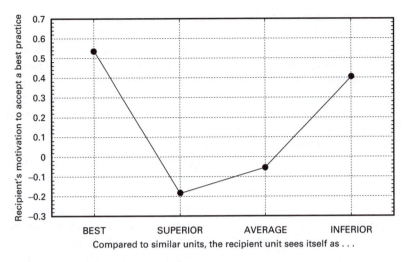

Figure 8.1 *The revised Not Invented Here syndrome*

many candidate recipient units, the one to which the transfer will be attempted first. Considerations may involve the need to secure a quick win, minimize the risk involved, maximize potential gains, or create a credible example, as well as the potential for learning.

A key consideration, regardless of the specific goal, is whether or not the recipient is motivated to absorb knowledge from the outside. The rule of thumb, derived from the often-called Not Invented Here syndrome, suggests that the more favourable the self-assessment of a unit the less inclined it will be to accept practices from other sister units. For example, Porter says that '[i]f business units have been industry leaders or pioneers ... they often resist any move toward joint efforts with sister units' (1985:390). One might add 'let alone accept best practices from sister units'. Following this logic, inferior units should always be the most motivated recipients for a transfer, because they need to improve and can't do so by themselves. Best units, following such logic, should be the least motivated.

The findings confirm this logic but with a twist. As can be seen in Figure 8.1, the 'NIH logic' holds for all but the best units. For all other units, reticence to adopt best practices is, as expected, inversely related to how favourable the unit's self-assessment is. For the best units, however, this logic does not hold. Units that see themselves as best had little reticence to receive external best practices. As a matter of fact, these units seemed as motivated as those units that rank themselves as inferior.

It is possible that the secret of such units for being and remaining the best is that they don't need to prove themselves anymore. Their willingness and ability to learn are what help them become and remain the best. This revised NIH logic means that not only inferior units, but also the best units of the organization could be natural candidates for the first transfer because either is likely to be a highly motivated recipient.

A transfer to a 'best' unit is probably a good choice when a quick win is desired or when risk of failure must be minimized. Best units are likely to be the most resourceful, able and visible units of the organization. Thus, the probability for success is higher and if those units benefit from the transfer, their success will be visible. However, a transfer to such units may result only in an incremental gain, and their success may not necessarily mean that transfers to inferior units will succeed.

For these reasons, when a large improvement, a credible example or when learning is the most important consideration, inferior units are probably a better choice. The potential for improvement is likely to be large. Furthermore, because these units are typically less resourceful and able, implementation is likely to encounter severe problems, which will provide numerous occasions for learning. This learning is likely to be valuable for subsequent transfers. Furthermore, a transfer that succeeds despite all these problems is a credible example of the robustness of the practice, and thus hesitation and reservation in other potential recipients is more likely to vanish, easing subsequent transfers.

If more than one transfer is to be attempted simultaneously then both the best and the inferior unit could be chosen for the first transfer. This, however, may come at the cost of diluting the attention that the source could give to each recipient. On the other hand, it may sometimes be necessary to begin a transfer simultaneously to several units, often 15–30 per cent of the total number of potential units, for the transfer efforts to gather critical mass.

Thus, the initiation of a transfer involves a number of dilemmas that must be resolved, taking into consideration the multiple characteristics of each transfer situation.

Senior management intervention and stickiness

Senior management has several options to intervene in the sharing of their corporation's own best practices. Sometimes, the urge to drastically reduce wasteful duplication of effort or to increase the use of existing, clearly superior, practices may precipitate direct interventions in specific transfer projects. On the other hand, demands on senior management time may limit their ability to get involved in a specific transfer. And even when time and availability are not constraints, a closer level of involvement may not necessarily reduce stickiness. Thus, the decision to intervene requires a choice with regards to the extent of the intervention. Thus, for example, specific transfers could be mandated, strongly suggested, favoured, presented as optional or simply left to unfold spontaneously.

The impact of the degree of intervention of senior management – i.e. the lack of autonomy of the participants in the transfer to decide whether or not

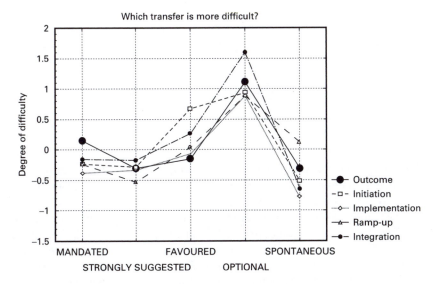

Figure 8.2   Senior Management Intervention and Stickiness

to do the transfer – on the degree of difficulty experienced in the transfer was examined using the findings of the survey. As Figure 8.2 suggests, 'Strongly suggested' or entirely 'Spontaneous' transfers were found to experience the lowest degree of difficulty. In contrast, 'Optional' transfers were found to experience the highest level of difficulty.

These findings imply that it is easier to transfer best practices with senior management approval, support and commitment than without it. They imply also that all four phases of transfer are easier when there is a committed champion. Transfers that are mandated or strongly suggested will typically have the backing of senior management. Transfers that happen spontaneously are likely to be driven by committed champions. Optional transfers seem to be stuck in the middle, in that they are unlikely to have strong backing from senior management, nor will they have a committed champion. Such transfers seem, on average, to be the most difficult ones to implement.

Note

1. The term diachronic is borrowed from linguistics to suggest contrasts between earlier and later moments of an activity. See Barley (1990) for a discussion of the nuances of the differences in the meaning of the terms diachronic and longitudinal.

9

Summary and Conclusion

The call for this study stemmed from an enduring puzzle. Dick Walton, from Harvard Business School, first called attention to it in the 1960s. In the 1990s, William Buehler, from Xerox, confirmed its presence when he declared his frustration to *Fortune* magazine: 'You can see a high-performance factory or office, but it just doesn't spread. I don't know why.' Indeed, the success of NUMMI, of Saturn at General Motors, of IBM's PC division are visible. Visible as well is the lack of internal diffusion of those practices. In concluding this book, it is perhaps the time to ask: what can we now say about the phenomenon?

The short answer is that we have new clues for how to rethink prevailing wisdom about why best practices may not spread. Conventional wisdom blames incentives, i.e. motivational barriers, almost exclusively. The statistical findings, however, point to knowledge-related barriers rather than to motivation-related barriers as the main culprit.

After briefly summarizing the study, its findings and their significance for research, I elaborate this main conclusion.

Summary

This book reports the findings of an empirical investigation into the nature and sources of the barriers to the transfer of best practice within the firm. When transfers of knowledge are sticky (i.e. difficult), a firm is unable to appropriate the full value of the rent from its knowledge. To this extent, stickiness in the transfer of best practice represents a critical performance problem for the firm. This study conceptualizes, operationalizes and assesses the relationship between stickiness and its predictors.

A sticky transfer is eventful. Eventfulness is assessed from the outcome of a transfer or by detecting events during the initiation, implementation, ramp-up and integration phases of the transfer. Stickiness originates from characteristics of the knowledge transferred, the source, the recipient and the context where the transfer occurs.

Thus, stickiness can be predicted by analysing the knowledge to be transferred or by analysing characteristics of the situation in which the transfer will occurs. Two characteristics of the knowledge transferred – causal ambiguity and unprovenness – and seven characteristics of the situation – a source that lacks motivation or is not perceived as reliable, a recipient that lacks motivation, absorptive capacity or retentive capacity, a barren organizational context and an arduous relationship between source and recipient – contribute to stickiness. The resulting framework has two sets of constructs. One set of constructs consists of five outcome and process-based measures of stickiness. The other set of constructs consists of nine measures of the origins of stickiness based on characteristics of the knowledge and of the transfer situation.

The study points to the importance of three major sources of stickiness: absorptive capacity, causal ambiguity and the quality of the relationship between source and recipient. Retentive capacity, when interpreted as the height of the unlearning barrier, also looms large. All of these origins of stickiness seem to dominate the motivation of the source and of the recipient as potential origins of stickiness. Yet, the analysis of the process measures in Chapter 7 suggests that factors other than those four, such as the perceived reliability of the source, may dominate specific stages of the process.

The conceptual framework developed in Chapters 3–5, illustrated in Chapter 6 and tested in Chapter 7 should help understand how a transfer happens, what difficulties are likely to be experienced at each stage and some structural correlates of those difficulties. In addition, some of the measures developed for the theoretical constructs of the framework could be used selectively to refine our understanding of practical facets of the phenomenon.

Significance

This study is, to my knowledge, one of the most extensive systematic studies of transfer of practices within organizations, and among the first to seek explicitly the perceptions of the source, the recipient and that of an external observer of the transfer. The findings should be relevant to those settings where the main concern is leveraging existing practices.

This study comes at a time when researchers studying the diffusion and transfer of complex technical knowledge have begun to seriously question the usefulness of a communications perspective for the study of knowledge transfer. For example, Attewell (1992) explained the limited explanatory power of studies of the diffusion of in-house business computing by arguing that technical know-how underlying such practices is relatively immobile, and therefore transfers of that kind of knowledge are often slow, difficult and incomplete (read sticky), forcing the recipient to reinvent and learn by doing. He suggested that the communication thinking underlying those studies is more appropriate for studying signalling than for studying the movement of such complex technical knowledge, and concluded that 'using an imagery of information transfer for technical knowledge is therefore unwise: it obscures more than it enlightens' (1992:6). Attewell proposed an alternative 'Knowledge Barrier Institutional Network' approach, in which supply-side institutions, such as service bureaus for business computing, play a central role in mitigating knowledge barriers to transfer that are encountered in the initial stages of the diffusion of such practices.

Attewell's argument hinges on the assumption that the adopter must make a special effort to learn a new practice. The greater such effort, the more important are supply-side institutions, such as a corporate information systems department, that can hold the hands of the user through the initial steps, thus significantly reducing the amount of learning that must precede successful adoption. Attewell thus implies that the lack of absorptive capacity of the adopter or recipient must be a major source of stickiness.

The findings of this study not only lend support but also help refine and elaborate Attewell's argument. First, the strong positive effect that lack of absorptive capacity has on stickiness suggests that recipients of knowledge, even when situated in the same institutional environment, may be more or less successful in bypassing knowledge barriers with the help of supply-side institutions, depending on their absorptive capacity. That is because absorptive capacity, as conceptualized and measured, reflects not only the adopter's ability to apply new knowledge but also to draw on outside expertise. Second, the positive impact that an arduous relationship between source and recipient of knowledge has on stickiness suggests that social ties act as conduits for knowledge, and that re-invention and learning-by-doing may not necessarily be a reflection of the technical complexity of the knowledge transferred. Instead they may stem partly from social factors that affect the quality of social ties, such as the recipient's need to maintain status, preserve identity and ownership, or make the application of new knowledge less threatening (Buttolph, 1992:464; Rice and Rogers, 1980:508–9). Third, the strong and positive effect that retentive capacity (which proxies routinized prior knowledge) has on stickiness suggests that, to surmount the knowledge barrier, the recipient has not only to reinvent or learn-by-doing the missing or incomplete parts of new knowledge, but that it also may have to make an deliberate effort to unlearn prior practices. Finally, Attewell, by emphasizing the knowledge barrier and the institutional network, seems to downplay the importance of the motivation of the source and of the recipient. The findings of this study suggest that both of these motivational factors are relatively less important than knowledge-related ones, but not to the point that they could be ignored, because they do matter, i.e. predict stickiness, sometimes in non-obvious, counter-intuitive ways.

The findings of this study support Attewell's basic argument and suggest three possible extensions. The first consists of exploring the moderating effect that absorptive capacity may have on the effectiveness of the supply-side institutions. An adopter with high absorptive capacity may require less support. The second extension consists of considering the impact of social factors, such as the motivations of the adopter, in addition to that of technological factors as possible determinants of the need to reinvent and learn-by-doing. The third extension consists of the introduction of a mirror-image barrier, the unlearning barrier, as another important determinant of the role of supply-side institutions. In addition to accompanying the adopter in taking the first steps with a new practice, supply-side institutions can specialize in helping the adopter to unlearn, discard and eliminate existing practices to accelerate the adoption process of new ones. Hence, this study, which is admittedly informed by an 'imagery of information transfer', illuminates some of what Attewell has left obscure – illustrating how a communication perspective could usefully complement other perspectives to the study of knowledge transfer.

From a conceptual standpoint, it should be noted that the notion of barriers to rent appropriation is a logical extension to the notions of barriers to entry, mobility and imitation. Indeed, when one takes the outsider perspective to any of these barriers, all of them are barriers to rent appropriation. Barriers to entry impede outsiders from appropriating monopoly rents accruing collectively to members of an attractive industry, and barriers to mobility also impede outsiders from appropriating monopoly rents accruing collectively to members of an attractive industry group (Porter, 1980). Barriers to imitation impede the appropriation of monopoly, Ricardian or Schumpeterian rents accruing to the owner of scarce assets. Barriers to rent appropriation, as defined in this book, prevent firms from appropriating rents from their own stock of knowledge. The firm is now an outsider to its own knowledge and to its rent-generating potential.

Thus the notion of barriers to rent appropriation adds to the natural progression of explanations for the sustainability of superior performance in the strategic management field. The durability of rents hinges not only on the presence of barriers to imitation but also on the absence of barriers to rent appropriation. Thus lack of persistent supra-normal profits may result from the absence of isolating mechanisms, or from the inability of the firm to appropriate rents from scarce assets in spite of the existence of isolating mechanisms, because of barriers to rent appropriation.

The above observation suggests how the findings afford additional insight into a seemingly fundamental strategic dilemma in the exploitation of superior knowledge.

Winter (1987) argued that a company could enhance the value of a certain stock of knowledge by rapidly expanding its use within the company or by entering licensing agreements or partnerships with other companies. To pursue any of these options, however, a company has to facilitate the transfer of that knowledge, by articulating and simplifying it, by disclosing underlying knowledge and by packaging it in a useful bundle. These actions, however, make it more difficult to protect knowledge from imitation by other firms. Thus, in exploiting knowledge a company faces a dilemma. As Winter explains, '[f]eatures that restrain involuntary transfer tend to inhibit voluntary transfer; likewise, actions undertaken to facilitate voluntary transfer may facilitate involuntary transfer also' (1987:174). Facilitating transfers of unique knowledge to expand the scope of its use makes imitation more likely, and risks reducing rather than increasing the overall value of that knowledge to the firm. Thus, exploiting knowledge through rapid internal or external expansion could be a double-edged sword.

Zander (1991) put Winter's contention to empirical scrutiny in the context of voluntary and involuntary dissemination of technology by Swedish multinational enterprises. In cooperation with Bruce Kogut, Zander developed four measures of constructs that could affect the transferability of the knowledge of the firm: codifiability, teachability, complexity and system dependence. In the empirical analysis, they found that none of these factors, nor the number of internal transfers of the technology, affected the probability that the technology would be imitated by a certain time. This, they concluded, challenged the assertion that voluntary and involuntary dissemination of technology were mirror-images of the same problem. In contrast, Zander found that actions that firms undertook to preserve secrecy, such as continuing to develop the technology, using proprietary equipment and making a special effort to retaining key employees, did impact the timing and likelihood of imitation.

The results of this study may help explain these findings. Indeed, causal ambiguity and proven knowledge, though important, are not the sole determinants of stickiness. Thus, it would seem that effective imitation depends also on the absorptive capacity of the imitator, the capacity of that imitator to unlearn the use of prior formally routinized knowledge[1] and on whether a good-quality relationship exists between the possessor of knowledge and the imitator. It seems that even after completely unlocking the secrets of superior knowledge, a prospective imitator may need to surmount other formidable barriers to imitation. This may explain Zander's findings because continually developing the technology, using proprietary equipment and retaining key employees could be reinterpreted as ways for the possessor of knowledge to preserve and enhance its own absorptive capacity. Voluntary and involuntary transfers of knowledge thus need not be tightly coupled phenomena. Barriers to rent appropriation could be reduced without necessarily reducing the effectiveness of inter-firm isolating mechanisms.

Finally, the tangible facet of stickiness manifests itself, for example, in practical difficulties experienced while transferring best practices inside the firm. The results suggest that prepared recipients, and an intimate relationship between source and recipient, go a long way in reducing barriers to transfer best practices. Additionally, the findings suggest that a developed retentive capacity for an existing practice is a barrier for the transfer of a new practice. Thus, it is not only the switch from self-reliance to reliance on others that impedes transfer, but also the routinization of prior practices, possibly received in a previous transfer.

This in turn suggests that there are lower bounds as well as upper bounds to an effective pace of organizational change. If the pace of change is too fast, change doesn't get implemented. But if it is too slow, it permits the development of excess retentive capacity, which becomes in itself a barrier for further change.

Lastly, to the extent that horizontal transfers of knowledge broaden organizational learning (Huber, 1991), the results suggest some attributes of the learning organization. The learning organization is characterized by prepared and motivated sub-units which are intimately connected, and that either at the sub-unit level or at the company level there exists the necessary processes and norms to unlearn prior knowledge. In such an organization, useful productive knowledge is broadly put to use and transfers of knowledge are simply non-events.

Conclusion: not just incentives

One may wonder about the generality of Mr Buehler's statement. Indeed, it is not always easy to spot a high-performance factory or office. In many cases, it is not so easy to 'tell apart good from bad' because sometimes our understanding of organizational practice is simplistic, distorted, superstitious, superficial or simply nonexistent.

What makes Mr Buehler's complaint increasingly relevant, however, is that in many companies it *is* becoming increasingly possible to tell apart good from bad. More and more companies are gaining enhanced understanding of their own practices and are able to develop useful measures through quality, re-engineering or benchmarking initiatives. Companies that remain wholly innocent of avoidable deficits in performance are rapidly becoming a minority. One may downplay the generality of the problem by arguing that perhaps only at Xerox, a pioneer of quality and benchmarking, and a small number of other large companies, is Mr Buehler's statement correct today. Yet, even if that were true, more companies are reaching Xerox's current stage. Reality is fast approaching Mr Buehler's description.[2]

For those companies already at Xerox's stage, Mr Buehler's statement is hardly news. Painfully aware of this reality, they blame it on inter-divisional jealousy, on the lack of incentives, lack of confidence, low priority, lack of buy-in, a heavy inclination to re-invent the wheel or to plough twice the same fields, refusal of recipients to do exactly what they are told, resistance to change, lack of commitment, turf protection and many other manifestations of what seem to be part of the popular definition of the NIH syndrome. Indeed, many practitioners would readily vow to this explanation.

Researchers who have looked at the phenomenon from a general management perspective seem to agree with the dominant view of practitioners. For example, Michael Porter notes, in line with Mr Buehler's statement, that 'the mere hope that one business unit might learn something useful from another is frequently a hope not realized' (1985:352). He explains that '[b]usiness units acting independently simply do not have the same incentives to propose and advocate strategies based on interrelationship as do higher level managers with a broader perspective'. He blames both the recipient, who can 'rarely be expected to seek out know-how elsewhere in the firm', and also the source, who 'will have little incentive to transfer [its know-how], particularly if it involves the time of some of their best people or involves proprietary technology that might leak out' (1985:368).

Porter's diagnosis is unequivocal: '[u]nless the motivation system reflects these differences [in perspective], it will be extremely difficult to get business units to agree to pursue an interrelationship and to work together to implement it successfully. Instead they become embroiled in fruitless negotiations over the allocation of shared costs or over procedures for sharing revenue.' As if re-inforcing the centrality of incentives, Goold *et al.* (1994:176) argue that enlightened, self-interested business-unit managers will exert their implicit veto rights on opportunities for knowledge sharing that they personally find unattractive.

The list of sources of impediments that follow from this conventional wisdom amounts to motivation writ large. Although in some cases, complex practices or problems of communication are mentioned, in most cases resistance to transfers is blamed on benefits that are or appear asymmetric, and on corporate incentive plans that indirectly penalize managers for pursuing transfers by not offering any positive incentive. To complicate things, corporate management's impetus to solve these problems by engineering incentives, the only seemingly available solution, is dampened by the fear of tampering with decentralization – to quell the entrepreneurial spirit of business units, to complicate the management of the organization by treating business units differently, to rely on subjective measures of performance and to provide excuses for poor performance. Faced with these considerations, many opt to leave the situation as it is rather than interfere with the organization. Maybe that's why the phenomenon has persisted for such a long time.

The respondents of the survey, when asked to describe the single most important difficulty, confirmed NIH, i.e. the lack of motivation on the part of the recipient, as the predominant source of difficulty. However, they also advanced many other non-motivational factors. Their answers are summarized in Figure 9.1.

A sample of the 80 answers classified as recipient motivation reads: acceptance by users, acceptance by staff; convincing staff to implement; and getting over the barrier of 'not invented here'. A sample of the 60 answers classified as absorptive capacity reads: change in mindset; becoming knowledgeable; coping with the new training methodology; developing equipment and process; hiring the right people; management training; relative inexperience of recipient; understanding a different approach to the market; and locating the process owner. A sample of the 18 answers classified as causal ambiguity reads: lack of documentation; metrics identification; nobody in the company fully understood the concept; and communication of a complex process in a simple manner. Finally, a sample of the

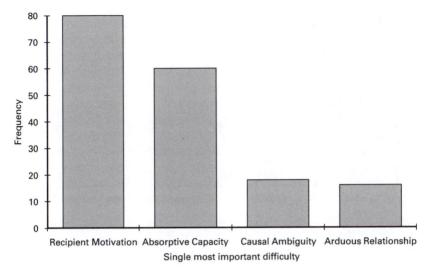

Figure 9.1   Single Most Important Barriers as Perceived by Managers

16 answers classified as relationship reads: distance; lack of communication; lack of open communication; and language problems.

When evaluated against this backcloth of conventional wisdom, the statistical findings of this study suggest several conclusions. First of all, what was called the conventional logic of NIH is crude. The best units of the organization do not seem to abide to that logic (see Chapter 8). Furthermore, contrary to common belief, highly motivated parties can be hazardous (see the discussion of statistical results in Chapter 7).

Perhaps the biggest surprise from the findings is that motivation factors are superseded by knowledge-related factors. The statistical analysis summarized in Figure 9.2[3] confirms the attributions of the survey respondents except for a single but telling detail. The motivation of the recipient ranks fourth in importance, not first. The motivation of the source ranks even lower.

The three most important barriers, i.e. lack of absorptive capacity of the recipient, causal ambiguity and the arduousness of the relationship, can all be interpreted as knowledge-related barriers. Indeed, absorptive capacity is a function of the knowledge endowment of the recipient prior to the transfer, causal ambiguity is a measure of the depth of knowledge or irreducible uncertainty faced by the recipient and the quality of the relationship affects the ability of a recipient in need to acquire required knowledge, i.e. the relationship acts as a conduit for knowledge. These knowledge-related barriers dominate statistically the motivation-related barriers.

These findings are suggestive, not definitive. But they cannot be ignored. Except for the motivation barrier, the statistical ranking of all the other three barriers matches the one emerging from the open-ended answers,

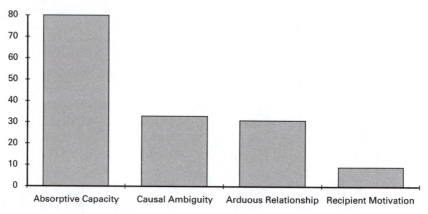

Figure 9.2   Relative Importance of Barriers based on the Statistical
Analysis

suggesting that conventional wisdom may be influencing respondents to overplay the role of motivation. Furthermore the findings are consistent with testimonies of modern organizational practice (e.g. Bartlett and Ghoshal, 1993), where initiative is delegated to line management and where one of middle management's most important roles is to foster horizontal linkages between sub-units, thus enhancing relationships. Perhaps one unspoken reason for the spreading of Total Quality Management (TQM), and related tools that stress management by fact rather than conjecture, is the imperative to increase understanding of organizational practice (reduce causal ambiguity) and empower units to improve on their own. TQM works only if all the organization is conversant in its methods and techniques. When that happens, organizational units are equipped to learn and improve on their own. Recipients have developed or are on the way to developing enhanced absorptive capacity.

At the very least, these findings invite us to pause and rethink conventional wisdom. To the extent that the results hold, they are heralding the need to redirect both research and practice. Judging from what I have observed and what is available in press, managers regularly bump against the baffling complexity of incentives. The thirst for novel and, for a change, effective solutions remains intact. Research invokes human pathologies to explain puzzling deviations from economic logic. Even though anomalies are acknowledged as increasingly large residuals in our explanations of social phenomena, they are still sidelined as they do not easily yield to statistical scrutiny. Structural, knowledge-related factors are still underplayed in practice, and are largely unexplored in theory.

Perhaps what impedes the working of enlightened self-interest, as Goold *et al.* (1994) would explain the absence of best practice spreading, is not so much a problem of self-interest. In times when organizational learning is rapidly becoming a competitive imperative and competition is hotting up, few business units can still afford to re-invent everything on their own. Hence we are bound to witness a change in norms where self-interest actually favours learning from others. This, for example, could be the outgrowth of the cultural shift that occurred at General Electric, where Jack Welch's Boundary-less Organization fostered a 'We Can Learn From Anyone' culture, a culture that stimulates innovative adaptation's of others' ideas through the rallying cry of 'stealing shamelessly' excellent ideas that are not trademarked, patented or proprietary.

As exchanges of knowledge become increasingly commonplace, norms of *quid pro quo* will make sharing a part of the behaviour that is taken for granted. Although this might mitigate the problem of self-interest for both the source and for the recipient it will not, however, mitigate the problem of enlightenment. In a fast-paced world, the value of existing knowledge and ideas diminishes quickly and therefore enlightenment has to be continually refreshed. In such a reality, the sophisticated engineering of incentives will prove increasingly ineffective to solve the puzzle highlighted by Mr Buehler. Solving that puzzle will require acknowledging actively the presence and subtlety of knowledge-related factors. It is perhaps such broadening of scope from an exclusive focus on incentives towards the other subtleties of knowledge management that may hold the key to resolve Mr Buehler's frustration.

Notes

1. Henderson and Clark (1990) make a similar point. They explain that the peculiar competitive pattern that characterized the photolitographic industry resulted from incumbents' inability to unlearn routinized architectural knowledge from their own successful innovation in the past, making them incapable of imitating effectively the architecture of superior technologies offered by competitors.

2. The American Productivity and Quality Center has begun tracking closely the phenomenon. What they have observed resembles Mr Buehler's eight-year-old formulation of the problem. In the words of Dr Carla O'Dell, director of the APQC: 'there is a lot of effort at identification but still very little implementation.'

3. This graph was constructed by squaring the canonical weights from the canonical correlation analysis in Chapter 7. Because of its anomalous sign, the weight of the coefficient of retentive capacity, although larger than the one of recipient motivation, is not in the graph.

Appendix 1: Research Design

This appendix describes the research design. Barriers to the transfer of best practice were studied in firms that attempted to transfer best practice, considered it important and found it was difficult. The unit of analysis is the transfer. Seeking robustness, the research process comprised two phases of data collection – an intensive phase and an extensive phase. The intensive phase consisted of in-depth clinical examination of transfers of best practice within three firms. The extensive phase consisted of a two-step large-sample survey. This appendix describes briefly the setting of the intensive phase, the data set assembled during the extensive phase, the process of analysis and the results.

The research process

The research question (Why might best practice not spread?) was used to specify the kind of organization to be approached in this research. Two heuristics were used to identify instances of such organizations. Reckoning that all research methods are flawed, though each differently (McGrath, 1982; Weick, 1989), a combination of two complementary research methods was used to increase the robustness of the research design. An intensive, in-depth clinical investigation of transfers in three companies was followed by an extensive, large-sample survey. Given the state of knowledge of the phenomena at the time it seemed adequate to begin the inquiry using intensive methods. The transfer was selected as the unit of analysis. Figure A1.1 summarizes graphically the research process.

Kind of organization

Given the research question, organizations of particular theoretical interest are active in transferring best practice and find this activity important and difficult. Best practices may not spread because firms are unaware of their own best practices, and also because, far from being automatic, the transfer of best practices inside the firm is restrained by difficulty. However, in firms that do not attempt to transfer best practice, the study of difficulty is corrupted by this lack of attempt. This is why the sampling framework focuses exclusively on those firms that attempt to transfer best practices internally. Until recently, these firms were rare. Recently, however, the transfer of best practices inside the firm has been stimulated by the diffusion of modern management techniques, such as TQM, that stress measurement and management by fact. Thus the study of such firms is now possible.

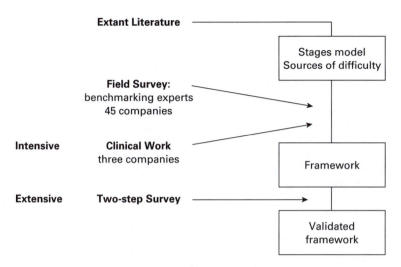

Figure A1.1 *The research process*

Selection heuristics

Two heuristics were used to identify theoretically relevant firms. One such heuristic was to seek large best-in-class firms that have small MES (Minimum Efficient Scale). Examples of such firms are fast food chains such as McDonald's or retail banks such as Banc One. These firms have many similar operating units that could readily benefit from sharing best practices and thus have strong incentives to replicate those best practices. The other heuristic was to approach firms that are active in competitive benchmarking. Active and successful benchmarking firms prepare thoroughly before contacting other firms for exchange (Balm, 1992). As part of this preparation they select carefully the questions they want to ask, the measures they want to use, and they assess the current performance of their units. Thus, an emerging norm in benchmarking is to benchmark inside the firm before attempting to benchmark outside the firm. Furthermore, once a superior practice is obtained through competitive benchmarking, it is reasonable to expect that firms will seek to leverage the benefits by diffusing that practice inside the firm. Thus, it was inferred that companies that do benchmarking will also be active in transferring best practices inside the firm. Contact with benchmarking firms was sought through the International Benchmarking Clearinghouse of the American Productivity and Quality Center and through the Council on Benchmarking of the Strategic Planning Institute (Main, 1992).

Besides relying on those two heuristics (small MES and active in competitive benchmarking) some firms were contacted directly based on their earned reputation as pioneers in the transfer of best practices inside the firm. One such firm was General Electric.

The transfer as unit of analysis

Although the unit of analysis is implicit in the research question, further clarification was needed to select the temporal and physical bounds of the research. In addition, it was desired that the unit of analysis conformed when possible to that of previous studies on the topic, and when it departed from those used in previous studies, it should be in clear and operationally defined ways. Preliminary evidence suggested that companies tend to organize the transfer of best practice in ways that resemble a project (Adler, 1990; Camp, 1989; Galbraith, 1990; Main, 1992; Teece, 1976; Tyre, 1991). Thus, it seemed sensible to select the unit of analysis of this research in terms of a 'project of transfer'. Furthermore, this study, in line with studies of diffusion of innovation, extended the definition of transfer to include the process of institutionalization of the new practice – unlike previous studies of technology transfer, which tend to define a transfer only up to the point where the technology has been successfully put to use in the recipient (Chew *et al.*, 1990; Teece, 1976).

Robust design: methodological triangulation

Every method offers a unique set of strengths and weaknesses and there is no absolutely best method (Jick, 1979; McGrath, 1982). The choice of any one method implies a set of trade-offs or dilemmas, e.g. accuracy at the expense of generality. Thus, the research combined an in-depth clinical investigation with a large-sample survey. The intensive, in-depth clinical examination of transfers sought to provide richness of contextual detail, permitting the grounded specification of constructs of the framework – both posited and emergent – in the language of the phenomena. The choice of in-depth clinical examination is justified by the form of the research questions (why?), because control over behavioural events is not required and because the study deals with contemporary events (Eisenhardt and Santos, 2001; Yin, 1979). An extensive, multiple-respondent survey based on a self-administered questionnaire was devised to validate the constructs and to evaluate empirically which are the most important relationships between the constructs of the framework. Triangulating between these two methods (Jick, 1979) permitted more dependable and generalizable conclusions to be reached from the study.

Maximizing quality of data

Special effort was directed to maximize the quality of data (Freeman, 1986; Groves, 1987), i.e. to access a theoretically relevant sample of firms and to minimize the incidence of measurement error. This was done under the belief that high quality of data would permit the selection of a robust and easily communicable method of analysis. The actions taken to maximize quality of data are method-specific and are therefore described in the method-specific sections below.

Getting started

An initial conceptual framework was devised as preparation for the data collection phase. This framework, largely based on a broad survey of academic literature and available press about the phenomena, provided an initial description of the process of transfer and of the sources of difficulty to the transfer of best practices. The framework guided the preparation of interview protocols, the questionnaire for the survey and (in abridged format) helped explain to potential participants the approach taken in this study.

A broad field survey of firms was undertaken to learn the language of the phenomena, identify relevant issues and calibrate the initial conceptual framework. Companies were contacted using the heuristics described above. Initial contacts were made either with public relations offices or with individuals suggested by the International Benchmarking Clearinghouse. A list of companies contacted is given below:

3M	Hughes Aircraft
Allstate Insurance	ITT Aerospace
Amoco	JC Penney
AMP	Kaiser Permanente
Arthur Andersen	Kodak
AT&T	MASCOTECH
AT&T Paradyne	McDonald's, Canada
Banc One	Mead Corporation
Blue Cross Blue Shield of Florida	New York Life Insurance
Bristol Myers Squibb	Nova Corporation of Canada
British petroleum	Pacific Bell
Burmah Castrol	Phillips Petroleum
Chevron	Pillisbury
Citicorp	Price Waterhouse
Deere & Company	Shell
Digital Corporation	Solvay
EDS	Sprint
Ford	Square D
General Electric	Sun Health
General Motors	Tektronix
Harris Aerospace	The Prudential
Honeywell	US Air Force
HP	Xerox
IBM	

At least one person from each company was interviewed. In some cases initial interviews were followed by visits or by follow-up telephone interviews. During a visit the initial conceptual framework was presented. During follow-up interviews, a portion of the interview time was devoted to the interviewees' comments on the framework. This exploratory field survey permitted potential sites for the clinical work to be identified, and for the large-sample survey.

Intensive phase: in-depth clinical examination of transfers

Transfers of best practice were examined in three companies. This intensive, in-depth clinical examination of transfers aimed to provide a deeper understanding of the phenomena, i.e. to provide rich descriptions of the process of transfer, to provide rich descriptions of the difficulties experienced during that process and to suggest potential explanations for those difficulties. Design considerations addressed potential threats to the validity as well as to the reliability of the findings. Besides providing insights, the fieldwork revealed the language that practitioners use to discuss the transfer of best practice, revealed some of the issues surrounding the phenomena and helped calibrate and refine the conceptual framework used in the empirical analysis.

Design considerations

Seeking the ultimate goal of objectivity (Kirk and Miller, 1986), the design considerations involving the fieldwork aimed to increase the validity and the reliability of the findings.

Validity

Companies were selected according to the theoretical criteria outlined above. Following Pettigrew's advice I sought extreme situations, where the process of interest is 'transparently observable' (Eisenhardt, 1989). Extreme situations were clearly successful or clearly unsuccessful transfers. This emphasis on extreme situations was thought to ease comparative analysis of the transfers under study.

To increase the external validity, i.e. generalizability, of the fieldwork it was desirable to study many cases. To control for spurious influences, however, it seemed sensible to limit the number of companies studied and to maximize the number of transfers documented within each company. Nord and Tucker (1987) found the firm to be an important source of extraneous variance. In their sample, firms had different starting points, encountered different events during implementation and sought different ends. Another important potential source of erroneous variance is the practice itself. The same practice could be defined differently in different companies, and even within the context of the same company. Thus, it seemed necessary to study only one practice per firm and to obtain as many cases of transfer as possible for each practice studied. Because of these considerations, the clinical work was limited to only three companies and, initially, to only one practice per company.

To gain access to the companies and to identify the transfers for study, I approached staff-level offices as the entry point in data collection. These offices provided background material and identified key informants. Key informants were the first persons interviewed. Interviews lasted between two-and-a-half and three-and-a-half hours. After the interview, key informants had a clear idea of what type of information I was seeking and of the design considerations of the study, e.g. how to identify suitable practices. They then set out to identify adequate transfers to study, provided me with relevant documentation about those transfers and introduced me to other people who had played critical roles in the process of transfer. I then tried to interview every person involved with the transfers to maximize the validity of the explanations. Construct validation was obtained by feeding back a write-up of the findings to the companies and obtaining the consensus of all participants as to the fidelity with which the findings documented the process of the transfer.

Reliability

To increase the reliability of my findings I relied on a systematic protocol and on multiple data collection methods, such as interviews, observations and archival sources. The fieldwork protocol consisted of three questions: How did the transfer happen? What were the difficulties during the transfer? Where did those difficulties come from? Using archival data, I sketched the answers to these questions in advance. This enabled me to use the interview time efficiently by estimating in advance the time that should be devoted to each question and by allowing me to detect valuable information and probe respondents for precision and depth. Further, when respondents tended to focus on only a few aspects of the transfer, I used the initial conceptual framework to generate more specific questions to guide the questioning. For example, when asking about the sources of difficulty, if a respondent tended to focus only on the characteristics of the recipient, I requested them to think also about characteristics of the source, of the practice and of the context in which the transfer happened. As I progressed through the interviews, some categories became saturated (Eisenhardt, 1989; Glaser and Strauss, 1968). Thus, while initial interviewing 'snowballed' around the key informant, I selected further interviewees increasingly on the basis of the specific categories where data was still insufficient. Interviews became more and more specialized, and sacrificed breadth to explore issues in greater depth.

The settings, Rank Xerox, Banc One and CENTEL, are described in detail in Chapter 6.

Contribution of the intensive phase: descriptive richness, the language of the phenomena, conceptual insights

Besides providing descriptive richness, the intensive phase helped calibrate and refine the conceptual framework in preparation for the empirical analysis, it helped operationalize the constructs using the language of the phenomena and revealed important contingency variables.

Calibrating and refining the theoretical framework: two new constructs and an insight

Besides helping refine the definition of the milestones and the description of the activities that occur in between the milestones in the process of transfer, the fieldwork revealed two important sources of stickiness that were absent in the initial conceptual map. These were the pre-existing relationship between the source and the recipient, and the degree of provenness of the practice prior to the transfer. The relationship, once recognized as an important contextual variable, was connected to received theory. In contrast, the construct of provenness gained empirical meaning directly from the fieldwork, i.e. it is a grounded construct. Besides revealing the importance of these two constructs, the fieldwork also helped refine the meaning of stickiness. The notion of stickiness as the eventfulness of the transfer is a discovery from the fieldwork, and is well captured in the following quote from an interview: 'Historically we have done too good a job. [Transfers] become non-events. People even don't notice. There are different opinions of what is success and what is failure. For us a [transfer] succeeds when it is a non-event in the customer eyes.'

Contingency variables

Immersion in the phenomena revealed contextual aspects that are important determinants of the outcome of the transfer. One such contingency variable was whether
the transfer is mandated or is left to happen spontaneously. Furthermore, there
were many situations in which the practice was transferred to several recipients and
an important problem was to decide the order in which best practice was to be transferred to the different recipients. A third important contingency variable was who
initiated the transfer. A transfer could be initiated by the source, by the recipient or
by a third party (e.g. corporate). The impact and implications of some of these
contingency factors are explored further in a later chapter fully dedicated to the
managerial facets of the study.

Extensive phase: two-step large-sample survey

The link between stickiness and barriers was tested through a two-step questionnaire survey. Special effort was directed to maximize the quality of data (Freeman,
1986; Groves, 1987), i.e. to access a theoretically relevant sample of firms and to
minimize the incidence of measurement error. The resulting relatively high quality
of data permitted, in turn, the selection of a robust and easily communicable method
of analysis. The first step of the survey consisted of a feasibility test. The second
step of the survey was devised to test the conceptual framework. Figure A1.2 below
summarizes the design criteria for the survey.

Step one: *exploring feasibility, self-selection of companies*

The first step of the survey was devised as a feasibility test. This test allowed self-
selection of theoretically relevant companies and generated, for companies that

❷ **Selecting firms that transfer best practices**

  – Active benchmarkers or small MES

❷ **Balanced perspective at the project level**

  – Source, recipient and third-party perspective
  – Reach inside the firm

❷ **Two-step process**

  – Generating a list of transfers
  – Evaluating those transfers with a customized survey

❷ **Self-selection of companies**

  – Written statement of commitment to the project
  – Visible coordinator appointed by senior management
  – Ability to provide list of transfers

Figure A1.2   *The survey*

cleared it successfully, a list of transfers to study and a list of parties involved in those transfers (i.e. of respondents). As explained earlier, two heuristics were used to identify theoretically relevant firms. One heuristic was to seek firms which were active in competitive benchmarking and the other was to approach best-in-class firms with many small-scale comparable operations, e.g. retail banks or fast-food chains.

To identify active benchmarkers, the International Benchmarking Clearinghouse[1] of the American Productivity and Quality Center in Houston, Texas was approached. After careful scrutiny, this institution endorsed the survey and brought it to the attention of its members. More than 2000 copies of a one-page description of the survey were mailed to the IBC membership – around 200 companies at that time. Additional firms with multiple small-scale operations were contacted individually.

To pass the feasibility test, companies had to submit a written statement of commitment to the project signed by a senior executive. This executive was requested to nominate a visible coordinator for the survey. The coordinator would scrutinize the pilot questionnaire, coordinate the administration of the final questionnaire and act as liaison with the researcher regarding any other aspect of the project. The first task for the nominated coordinators was to provide a list, and a succinct description, of the practices that their company wished to study. They were also requested to provide a list of actual transfers of those practices. For each transfer in that list, coordinators were requested to identify a representative of the source unit, a representative of the recipient unit and a representative of a third party, familiar with the transfer but not a member of the source or the recipient. These representatives would become the actual respondents to the questionnaire survey for that transfer.

The exchange of information was regulated by the benchmarking code of conduct devised by the International Benchmarking Clearinghouse. Participating companies, as compensation for their efforts (one-to-two person–month per company), were promised company-specific feedback. Over 60 companies expressed initial interest and initiated the feasibility test. Of the 60, 12 completed the first phase of the survey and 8 were admitted to the second phase of the survey.[2]

The first phase of the survey took six months to complete. In total, 184 transfers of 44 practices were identified, requiring 445 questionnaires.[3] To select 'practices' for this study, the coordinators were directed to search for transfers between peer units of important activities or processes, and to prefer those that showed evidence of difficulty during the transfer and of adaptation of the practice by the recipient. They were also instructed to rule out practices that could be performed by a single individual and favour exclusively those practices that required the coordinated effort of several individuals. These practical guidelines were devised to screen organizational activities that corresponded closely to the theoretical considerations involved in the replication of an organizational routine (Nelson and Winter, 1982).

Step two: testing the framework

The second step of the survey was devised to test the conceptual framework. The final sample encompassed 271 returned questionnaires, spanning 122 transfers of 38 practices,[4] making for a response rate of 61 per cent. This rate of response is similar to that obtained by the participating companies in their annual employee attitude survey. Yet, because the questionnaire had 255 items, five times as many as a typical employee attitude survey, and because it took on average one hour to complete

❷ **Participating Companies (8)**

AMP AT&T Paradyne, BP, Burmah Castrol, Chevron Corporation, EDS, Kaiser Permanente, Rank Xerox

❷ **38 technical and administrative practices**

technical: e.g. software development, drafting standards
administrative: e.g. ABC, upward appraisal

❷ **122 transfers**

❷ **sample size = 271**

110 sources, 101 recipients and 60 third parties

Figure A1.3   *The sample*

it, four times longer than a typical attitude survey questionnaire, the relatively high response rate suggests a high level of commitment by both respondents and coordinators. The sampling criteria sought to obtain a balanced perspective on each transfer by sending one questionnaire to the source, one to the recipient and one to a third party to the transfer. Regarding type of respondent, 110 questionnaires were received from sources units, 101 questionnaires from recipients and 60 from third parties. Harder to identify, third parties also proved less likely to return the questionnaire.[5] When they did return the questionnaire, they responded to fewer items than the source or the recipient did. Average item-non-response was lower than 5 per cent. On average 7.3 questionnaires were received for each practice studied. Figure A1.3 describes the sample.

In the design and administration of the questionnaire, everything feasible was attempted to prevent the incidence of measurement error (Nunnally, 1978). The questionnaire was formulated only after an extensive field survey of 45 large companies that were active in benchmarking, and an in-depth clinical investigation in three companies revealed the language of the phenomena and helped calibrate the theoretical framework of the study. Specialist advice was sought to secure a professional appearance to the questionnaire.

During one full month, the pilot questionnaire was pre-tested and refined, as recommended by Dillman (1978), with the help of all the participating companies, with the help of experienced academics and also with the help of respondents who volunteered to record in detail their reactions while filling in the questionnaire. All the coordinators and at least one other person from each of the participating companies reviewed the pilot questionnaire to ensure that the instructions were easily understood and that the questions were meaningful and clear. In addition, the coordinators were offered the possibility to add company-specific questions to the questionnaire. This option proved particularly effective to motivate them to cross-check closely their questions with those already in the questionnaire. Extensive awareness-building efforts inside the participating companies preceded the actual sending of the questionnaire. Coordinators, or a senior executive, wrote to all respondents in advance, explaining the purpose and importance of the study for the company and assuring confidentiality. A cover letter explaining the purpose of the questionnaire and guaranteeing confidentiality accompanied each questionnaire (see Appendix 2).

Finally, the cognitive load on the respondents was reduced by customizing each questionnaire using information collected during the first phase of the survey and by using a streamlined and intuitive set of scales. Source, recipient and third party received the same questionnaire. The generic words 'source', 'recipient', 'third party', 'practice' and 'company' were replaced by specific identifiers for each transfer, minimizing the need for the respondent to do mental translations. This customization, together with the company-specific questions, gave the impression that the survey was tailored specifically for each company, increasing the total buy-in into the process. To simplify the rules for scoring, a single, intuitive, five-point Likert-type scale was used for most questions. A five-point Likert scale, the minimum recommended by Cox (1980) and the most common for this type of scale (Babakus *et al.*, 1987), was preferred because it corresponded to standard practice within most of the participating companies, and because an explicit and consistent rule for scoring could be formulated.

Multi-item scales, simplicity in scoring

To ensure the reliability and validity of the measurement system, multi-item scales were developed for all constructs. The benefit of a multi-item scale is that 'individual item idiosyncrasies and fluctuations tend to cancel one another out' (Marsden, 1990:456), providing 'the primary way to make tests more reliable' (Nunnally, 1978:243). Little empirical precedent existed to develop most of these measures. To develop the scales, a broad and thorough literature review helped generate the initial constructs and the items to measure those constructs. The intensive phase helped fine-tune the choice of constructs, and provided the anchor to select the most relevant items for those constructs, given the empirical context of this study, i.e., intra-firm transfer of best practice. Items were also selected based on feedback obtained on the pilot questionnaire, and further refined using the full data set.

Simplicity in scoring was sought by relying almost exclusively on a single balanced five-point Likert-type scale that was relatively straightforward to master. The scale used was: **Y!** = 'Yes!', **y** = 'yes, but', **o** = 'no opinion', **n** = 'no, not really', **N!** = 'No!'. The total score for each scale was computed by adding the standardized scores (Nunnally, 1978).

The dependent variable and key independent variables are described below. Full text for the questionnaire is included in Appendix 5.

Dependent variables: stickiness as eventfulness of transfer

1. Outcome-based measure

The project will be on time, on budget and it will achieve the stated goals. Pick two out of the three. (Anonymous)

Stickiness was measured using a set of eight items corresponding to the so-called technical success indicators of a project (Pinto and Mantel, 1990; Randolph and Posner, 1988) – on time, on budget and a satisfied recipient. Deviation in timing was measured as departure from the initial plan in reaching key milestones – the start of the transfer, the first day the practice became operational at the recipient and achievement of satisfactory performance. For these three items the five possible answers were:

1. ADVANCED BY MORE THAN ONE MONTH
2. ADVANCED LESS THAN ONE MONTH
3. NOT RESCHEDULED
4. DELAYED LESS THAN ONE MONTH
5. DELAYED MORE THAN ONE MONTH

Two items measured departure of actual cost from expected cost on the source side and the recipient side. For these two items the five possible answers were:

1. MUCH (>30%) MORE THAN EXPECTED
2. SLIGHTLY MORE (<30%) THAN EXPECTED
3. AS EXPECTED
4. SLIGHTLY (<30%) LESS THAN EXPECTED
5. MUCH LESS (<30%) THAN EXPECTED

Finally, three items measured recipient's satisfaction. One item measured adjustment in the recipient's expectations after gaining experience with the practice. The possible answers for this question were:

1. DRAMATICALLY UPWARD
2. SLIGHTLY UPWARD
3. NO CHANGE
4. SLIGHTLY DOWNWARD
5. DRAMATICALLY DOWNWARD

Two items measured whether the recipient was satisfied with the quality of the practice and with the quality of the transfer. For these two items, the possible answers were:

1. VERY SATISFIED
2. SOMEWHAT SATISFIED
3. NEITHER SATISFIED NOR DISSATISFIED
4. SOMEWHAT DISSATISFIED
5. VERY DISSATISFIED

2. Process-based measures

Process-based measures aim to capture the degree of difficulty experienced at the different stages of the transfer, i.e. during initiation, implementation, ramp-up and integration. Micro-events first observed during the fieldwork or reported in the literature are formulated as statements which are true to a larger or smaller degree. Unless indicated, the answer is measured using the default scale (**Y!** Y O N **N!**). Each sentence in the description of the scales below corresponds to one item of the questionnaire.

Stickiness during the initiation phase (default scale) Ranking the performance of «company»'s units on their results on «practice» was straightforward. <u>Within «company»</u>, there existed consensus that «source» has obtained the best results with «practice». Compared to <u>external</u> benchmarks, «source» has obtained best-in-class results with «practice». «source» could easily explain how it obtained superior results with «practice». «source» could easily point to the key components of «practice». «source» was reluctant to share crucial knowledge and information relative to «practice». Distributing responsibility for the transfer between «source» and «recipient» generated much conflict. The transfer of «practice» from «source» to «recipient» was amply justified.

Stickiness during the implementation phase (default scale)   «recipient» recognized «source»'s expertise on «practice». The transfer of «practice» from «source» to «recipient» disrupted «source» normal operations. «recipient» could not free personnel from regular operations so that it could be properly trained. Communication of transfer-related information broke down within «recipient». «recipient» was able to recognize inadequacies in «source»'s offerings. «recipient» knew what questions to ask «source». «recipient» knew how to recognize its requirements for «practice». «recipient» performed unnecessary modifications to the «practice». «recipient» modified the «practice» in ways contrary to expert advice. «source» turned out to be less knowledgeable of the «practice» than it appeared before the transfer was decided. Much of what «recipient» should have done during the transfer was eventually completed by «source». «source» understood «recipient»'s unique situation. All aspects of the transfer of «practice» from «source» to «recipient» were carefully planned.

Stickiness during the ramp-up phase (default scale)   Initially «recipient» 'spoon fed' the «practice» with carefully selected personnel and raw material until it got up to speed. At first «recipient» measured performance more often than usual, sometimes reacting too briskly to transient declines in performance. Some people left «recipient» after having been trained for their new role in the «practice», forcing «recipient» to hire hastily a replacement and train it 'on the fly'. Some people turned out to be poorly qualified to perform their new role in the «practice», forcing «recipient» to hire hastily a replacement and train it 'on the fly'. The «practice» had unsatisfactory side effects which «recipient» had to correct. By altering the «practice», «recipient» created further problems which had to be solved. «recipient»'s environment turned out to be different from that of «source» forcing «recipient» to make unforeseen changes to «practice». Outside experts (from «source», other units, or external consultants) could answer questions and solve problems about their specialty but did not have an overall perspective on the «practice». Teams put together to help «recipient» to get up to speed with the «practice» disbanded because their members had to attend to other pressing tasks.

Stickiness during the integration phase (default scale unless indicated)   «recipient» has not yet solved all problems caused by the introduction of the «practice», because energy and resources were siphoned off by daily work pressures. Some of the 'temporary workarounds' devised to help «recipient» get up to speed became habitual. For the «practice» today, the roles are well defined. «recipient» personnel are content to play their roles in «practice». The appropriateness of performing the «practice» in «recipient» has been <u>explicitly questioned</u> after its introduction. «recipient» has reconsidered its decision to adopt the «practice». «recipient»'s expectations created during the introduction of the «practice» have been met. Individual values favour performing the «practice». It is clear why «recipient» needs the «practice». The justification for performing the «practice» at «recipient» makes sense. The activities accompanying the «practice» are: (*circle one option*) 1. OBVIOUSLY FUNCTIONAL 2. SOMEWHAT AGAINST THE GRAIN OF EXISTING WORK PRACTICES 3. ARBITRARY WITHOUT A BASIS IN REALITY.

Independent variables: origins of stickiness

The operationalization of the nine explanatory constructs – the two characteristics of the knowledge and the seven characteristics of the situation – is described in this section. Unless otherwise stated, the default scale is used.

1. Characteristics of the knowledge transferred

Causal ambiguity (default scale)   The limits of the «practice» are fully specified. With the «practice», we know why a given action results in a given outcome. When a problem surfaced with the «practice», the precise reasons for failure could not be articulated even after the event. There is a precise list of the skills, resources and prerequisites necessary for successfully performing the «practice». It is well known how the components of that list interact to produce «practice»'s output. Operating procedures for the «practice» are available. Useful manuals for the «practice» are available. Existing work manuals and operating procedures describe precisely what people working in the «practice» actually do.

Unproven knowledge (default scale unless indicated)   We had solid proof that «practice» was really helpful. «practice» contributes significantly to the competitive advantage of «company». For the success of «company», the «practice» is: 1. CRITICAL 2. VERY IMPORTANT 3. FAIRLY IMPORTANT 4. FAIRLY UNIMPORTANT 5. NOT IMPORTANT AT ALL.

2. Characteristics of the source

Source lacks motivation (binary items)   «Source» saw benefit in: measuring its own performance; understanding its own practices; sharing this understanding with other units; sharing the limits of this understanding with other units; assessing the feasibility of the transfer; communicating with «recipient»; planning the transfer; documenting «practice» for transfer; implementing «recipient»'s support systems; training «recipient»'s personnel; helping «recipient» troubleshoot; helping resolve recipient's unexpected problems; lending skilled personnel.

Source is not perceived as reliable (default scale, unless indicated)   «source» and «recipient» have similar Key Success Factors; «source»: 1. INVENTED THE «PRACTICE» 2. WAS

THE FIRST UNIT TO HAVE EXPERIENCE 3. RECEIVED PRACTICE FROM OTHER UNIT; «source» was able to accommodate the needs of «recipient» into «practice»; «source» had an hidden agenda; the superior results of the «source» were visible; remained stable; «source» possessed the necessary resources to support the transfer; «source» has a history of successful transfers.

3. Characteristics of the recipient

Recipient lacks motivation (binary items)   «Recipient» saw benefit in: measuring its own performance; comparing it with the performance of other units; understanding its own practices; absorbing «source»'s understanding; analysing the feasibility of adopting «practice»; communicating its needs to «source»; planning the transfer; implementing the systems and facilities for «practice»; assigning personnel full time to the transfer; assigning personnel to be trained in «practice»; understanding the implications of the transfer; troubleshooting «practice»; ensuring that its people knew their jobs; ensuring that its people consented to keep doing their jobs.

Recipient lacks absorptive capacity (default scale)   Members of «recipient» have a common language to deal with the «practice»; «recipient» had a vision of what it was trying to achieve through the transfer; «recipient» had information on the state-of-the-art of the «practice»; «recipient» had a clear division of roles and responsibilities to implement the «practice»; «recipient» had the necessary skills to implement the «practice»; «recipient» had the technical competence to absorb the «practice»; «recipient» had the managerial competence to absorb the «practice»; it is well known who can best exploit new information about the «practice» within «recipient»; it is well known who can help solve problems associated with the «practice».

Recipient lacks retentive capacity (default scale)   «Recipient» periodically retrains existing personnel on the «practice»; «recipient» has mechanisms to detect malfunctions of the «practice»; «recipient» regularly measures performance and corrects problems as soon as these happen; «recipient»'s personnel can predict how they will be rewarded for good performance in the «practice»; «recipient»'s personnel are provided with numerous opportunities to commit freely and publicly to perform their role; at «recipient» there is a clear focal point for the «practice».

4. Characteristics of the social context

Barren organizational context (default scale)   Existing performance measures of the «practice» are detailed enough to be meaningful. Performance measures of the «practice» are taken frequently enough to be timely. Performance measures of the «practice» from different units are easily comparable. «company» enforces company-wide standard policies with respect to the «practice». At «company» there is constant pressure to improve performance. It is easy to justify time spent visiting other units. To visit another unit, it is easy to justify travel expenses. At «company», improving performance by copying and adapting practices from other units is as legitimate as improving performance from own creativity. At «company», a unit that exposes those needs that it is unable to meet on its own looses status. At «company», a unit that exposes unresolved problems looses status. At «company», despite structural differences units can always learn from one another. Normally a best-in-class practice is most likely to be found outside «company». At «company», managers seem to prefer to use external sources of help and support even though they are more expensive and less useful. At «company», corporate pride and values encourage managers not to look outside for help or to share with the outside.

Arduous relationship   Communication between «source» and «recipient» is 1. VERY EASY 2. FAIRLY EASY 3. FAIRLY DEMANDING 4. VERY DEMANDING; collaboration between «source» and «recipient» is 1. SOUGHT ACTIVELY BY SOURCE 2. WELL RECEIVED BUT NOT SOUGHT ACTIVELY BY SOURCE 3. PREFERABLY AVOIDED BY SOURCE 4. OCCURS ONLY IF SOURCE HAS NO CHOICE; collaboration between «source» and «recipient» is 1. SOUGHT ACTIVELY BY RECIPIENT 2. IS WELL RECEIVED BUT NOT SOUGHT ACTIVELY BY RECIPIENT 3. IS PREFERABLY AVOIDED BY RECIPIENT 4. OCCURS ONLY IF RECIPIENT HAS NO CHOICE.

Statistical analysis and findings: introduction to the results of the extensive phase

The goal of the empirical analysis was to evaluate the empirical performance of the conceptual framework advanced in Chapters 4 and 5. This evaluation included gauging the performance of the measurement model, the empirical weight of each relationship and whether the association between variables conforms to predictions. Auxiliary information pertaining to the timing of the administration of the questionnaire is supplied to assist in the interpretation of the results. The performance of the measurement model is discussed in terms of convergent and discriminant validity. The correlation table between the explanatory constructs is then followed by a brief discussion of the overall plan for analysis.

Timing and assumptions

The questionnaires were administered between four and ten months after the studied practice was first put to use by the recipient. Figure A1.4 describes the distribution of the timing of administration of the questionnaire. All the variables were measured at that instant in time.

As a first approximation, the independent variables of the framework are assumed to be stable for the duration of the transfer. When this assumption holds the timing of the measurement of the independent variables is not critical and, by implication, there is no ambiguity about the causal direction of the studied relationships.

Clearly this assumption needs careful scrutiny and might not hold in all situations. Some variables, such as the motivation of the source, the motivation of the recipient or the nature of their relationship may evolve with the transfer as a

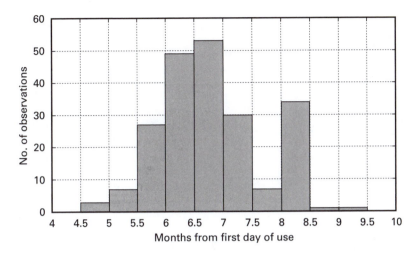

Figure A1.4   *Timing of the administration of the questionnaire*

consequence of ongoing interactions and thus, to some extent, be determined by the unfolding of the transfer. In this respect the observations from the fieldwork suggest that most of the fluctuations in these constructs tend to be confined to the initiation stage. Thereafter, fluctuations diminish significantly. Thus there is a latent problem of simultaneity which calls for caution in discussing causality and the meaning of the measured variables.

Leonard-Barton (1990a:259) found that measures of some of her constructs, which overlap with constructs developed in this study (e.g. 'Communicability') were sensitive to the point in time at which they were administered. Thus, she found it necessary to measure at a 'defined point' in time in order to make meaningful comparisons across transfers. The point of reference she used was the 'very first use of the technology in a routine production task'. She chose that point because it could be identified with a 'satisfactory degree of precision'. All questionnaires were completed within a narrow[6] band of between five and eight-and-a-half months after the first day of use of the transferred knowledge by the recipient. Comparison across transfers seems therefore largely warranted although the timing of the measurement should be considered when discussing and interpreting the findings.

Performance of the measurement model

Of particular concern is the performance of the measurement model. To assess the performance of the measurement model, convergent validity, i.e. reliability and uni-dimensionality, was evaluated for each construct (Gerbing and Anderson, 1988). For reliability, Cronbach Alpha is reported for each scale because this measure is believed to provide a lower bound for the reliability of a scale and is the most widely used measure (Nunnally, 1978). Uni-dimensionality was assessed through factor analysis and the computation of the Theta coefficient (Armor, 1974; Carmines and Zeller, 1979; Zeller and Carmines, 1980).

Table A1.1 *Performance of the measurement model*

Construct	Description	Cronbach alpha	Items	Valid N	Avg. Inter-item Correlation
Stickiness – Outcome	eventfulness of the transfer of knowledge (delay, budget overrun, satisfaction gaps)	.80	8	140	.34
Stickiness – Initiation	difficulties experienced prior to the decision to transfer	.74	8	241	.27
Stickiness – Implementation	difficulties experienced between the decision to transfer and start of actual use	.83	13	240	.28
Stickiness – Ramp-up	unexpected problems from the start of actual use until satisfactory performance obtained	.77	9	236	.28
Stickiness – Integration	difficulties experienced after satisfactory performance is achieved	.79	12	224	.25
Source lacks Motivation*	the motivation of the source unit to support the transfer	.93	13	271	.50
Source not perceived as Reliable	the degree to which the donor of the best practice is perceived as reliable	.64	8	210	.19
Recipient lacks Motivation*	the motivation of the recipient unit to support the transfer	.93	14	271	.48
Recipient lacks Absorptive Capacity	the ability of the recipient unit to identify, value and apply new knowledge	.83	9	252	.36
Recipient lacks Retentive Capacity	the ability of the recipient unit to routinize the use of new knowledge	.81	6	249	.43
Causal Ambiguity	depth of knowledge	.86	8	250	.45
Unproven Knowledge	degree of conjecture on the utility of the transferred knowledge	.67	3	251	.40
Barren Organizational Context	degree to which the organizational context supports the development of transfers	.77	14	247	.20
Arduous Relationship	the ease of communication and the intimacy of the relationship	.71	3	237	.46

*These scales are composed of binary items. Both scales qualify marginally as Guttman scales. The Guttman coefficient of reproducibility (CR) – computed according to Goodenough-Edwards (a more conservative) criterion for counting errors – is .84 for the Source Motivation scale and is .80 for the Recipient Motivation scale. Todd's coefficient of scalability (CS) is .72 for the Source Motivation scale and .63 for the Recipient Motivation scale. A scale with CR ≥ .90 and CS > .60 can be considered an adequate Guttman scale (McIver and Carmines, 1981:40–55).

Table A1.1 summarizes the performance of the measurement model. The constructs appear adequate in terms of their reliability, uni-dimensionality and discriminant validity. In terms of reliability, all but two scales have Cronbach alpha > 0.7, thus providing an adequate level of reliability for predictor tests and hypothesized measures of a construct (Nunnally, 1978:245–6). Two scales are marginally below this standard – 'Lack of Source Perceived Reliability' (.644) and 'Unproven Knowledge' (.67). The uni-dimensionality of all 10 scales received adequate support. The performance of the binary scales that measure motivation is particularly noteworthy. Both scales have Cronbach Alpha > 0.9 and both meet well the uni-dimensionality test. Furthermore, both scales qualify marginally for the Guttman criterion for scalability (McIver and Carmines, 1981).

Discriminant validity

This section explains the method used to evaluate the discriminant validity of the proposed measurement model and summarizes the result of the test. It should be noted that discriminant validity is a pairwise concern, not a simultaneous property of all constructs in a model. Thus, discriminant validity is evaluated by examining the observed correlation matrix of the constructs. If the correlation between constructs i and j is 1, i.e. if constructs i and j are perfectly correlated, the observed correlation should be $(i^{0.5})*(j^{0.5})$ where alpha$_i$ and alpha$_j$ are the reliability coefficients for these constructs. In practical terms, testing for discriminant validity entails computing the upper limit for the confidence interval of the observed correlation and testing that this limit is smaller than the maximum possible correlation between the scales as computed from their reliability coefficients (see Howell, 1987:121 for a critique of this approach, and Morrison, 1976:104–5 for the mathematics behind the approach). The upper limit of the confidence interval is given by the expression:

$$\text{upper limit} = \tanh(\tanh^{-1}(\rho) + z_{1/2}/(N-3)^{0.5})$$

where tanh is the hyperbolic tangent function, ρ is the observed correlation coefficient, $z_{1/2}$ is the upper 50 percentage points of the standard normal distribution function and N is the number of sample points used in the computation of the correlation. Using this method, discriminant validity was supported for all construct pairs up to a confidence level of p<.0001, except for the construct pair 'Source not perceived as Reliable' and 'Stickiness – Initiation', for which discriminant validity can be supported only up to p<.0012.

Correlation table

Table A1.2 presents the correlation for the variables. Correlations are computed with available data only; no substitutions were made for missing indicators. Accordingly, the number of cases varies between 196 and 271. The average number of cases is 235.

Analysis and results of the extensive phase

The analysis includes both multiple regression and canonical correlation. In order to analyse the impact of the barriers in each stages, four multiple regression

Table A1.2 *Pearson Product-Moment Correlation among variables (missing data deleted pairwise: Nmax = 271, Nmin = 196, Navg = 235)*

	1	2	3	4	5	6	7	8
Source lacks Motivation								
Source not perceived as Reliable	0.46							
Recipient lacks Motivation	0.48	0.34						
Recipient lacks Absorptive Capacity	0.07	0.27	0.39					
Recipient lacks Retentive Capacity	−0.11	0.09	0.18	0.62				
Causal Ambiguity	0.32	0.47	0.21	0.23	0.25			
Unproven Knowledge	0.27	0.33	0.17	0.16	0.08	0.43		
Barren Organizational Context	0.25	0.28	0.30	0.44	0.46	0.35	0.25	
Arduous Relationship	0.21	0.32	0.29	0.24	0.15	0.28	0.31	0.35

Shaded correlations are significant at $p < .05$

equations are developed. Each equation has one type of stickiness as a dependent variable. In each equation the nine barriers are the independent variables and several controls are included. In order to analyse the overall impact of barriers, the canonical correlation uses two sets of variables. The first set includes the four types of stickiness and the overall stickiness; the second set includes the nine barriers.

Results of the regression analysis

Table A1.3 displays the findings from the regression analyses run separately on each measure of stickiness column. The four models have significant explanatory power (adj. Rsq. $\geq .4$) for each of the process-based descriptors of internal stickiness.

Overall, the pattern of results is consistent with the general expectation that factors affecting the opportunity to transfer are more likely to predict difficulty during the initiation phase, whereas factors affecting the execution of the transfer are more likely to predict difficulty during implementation phases. In column I (Stickiness initiating) the coefficients of causal ambiguity (0.20, $p < .001$), unproveness of knowledge (0.27, $p < .001$) and lack of credibility (0.27, $p < .001$) are all highly significant and positive. In column II (Stickiness implementing) the coefficients of causal ambiguity (0.23, $p < .001$) and lack of recipient's absorptive capacity (0.47, $p < .001$) are highly significant and positive; the coefficients of lack of source's motivation (0.17, $p < .05$) and credibility (0.17, $p < .05$) and the coefficient of arduous relationship (0.16, $p < .05$) are significant and positive. In column III (Stickiness ramp-up) the coefficients of causal ambiguity (0.24, $p < .001$), of lack of source's credibility (0.24, $p < .001$), of lack of recipient's absorptive capacity (0.49, $p < .001$) and of barren context (0.21, $p < .001$) are highly significant and positive; conversely the coefficient of lack of recipient's retentive capacity (−0.43, $p < .001$) is equally significant but negative. In column IV (stickiness integrating) the coefficients of lack of recipient's motivation (0.19, $p < .001$) and absorptive capacity (0.45, $p < .001$) and the coefficient of barren context (0.21, $p < .001$) and arduous relationship (0.19, $p < .001$) are highly significant and positive.

The spontaneity of the transfer, as control, is initially significant with a negative sign (−0.16, $p < .05$ in column I; −0.10, $p < .10$ in column II).

Table A1.3 *Regressions of internal stickiness for each stage*

Variable	Standardized beta coefficients (t – value)			
	Stickiness Initiating (I)	Stickiness Implementing (II)	Stickiness Ramp-up (III)	Stickiness Integrating (IV)
Causal Ambiguity	0.20**	0.23**	0.24**	0.16*
	(2.74)	(3.32)	(3.39)	(2.50)
Unproven Knowledge	0.27**	0.11+	−0.09	−0.09
	(3.89)	(1.72)	(−1.23)	(−1.43)
Source lacks Motivation	0.07	0.17*	0.16*	0.06
	(0.92)	(2.33)	(2.21)	(0.97)
Source lacks Credibility	0.27**	0.17*	0.24**	−0.05
	(3.59)	(2.25)	(3.23)	(−0.76)
Recipient lacks Motivation	0.10	−0.07	−0.14*	0.19**
	(1.35)	(−0.95)	(−2.05)	(3.07)
Recipient lacks Absorptive Capacity	0.11	0.47**	0.49**	0.45**
	(1.37)	(5.87)	(6.08)	(6.07)
Recipient lacks Retentive Capacity	−0.01	−0.03	−0.43**	0.01
	(−0.10)	(−0.46)	(−5.73)	(0.20)
Barren Organizational Context	−0.04	−0.06	0.21**	0.21**
	(−0.55)	(−0.81)	(2.86)	(3.18)
Arduous Relationship	0.05	0.16*	0.07	0.19**
	(0.70)	(2.38)	(1.12)	(3.17)
Spontaneity	−0.16*	−0.10+	0.00	0.00
	(−2.53)	(−1.71)	(0.06)	(0.03)
Residual (I)		0.17**	0.11+	−0.10*
		(3.04)	(1.90)	(−1.99)
Residual (II)			0.30**	0.21**
			(5.22)	(4.17)
Residual (III)				0.16**
				(3.18)
R^2	0.46	0.54	0.56	0.68
Adj.-R^2	**0.42**	**0.51**	**0.52**	**0.64**
F	15.88	14.6	15.88	20.62
N	166	150	158	142

+p<.10; *p<.05; **p<.01

Results of the canonical correlation analysis

The results of the canonical correlation analysis are summarized in Figure A1.5.

Canonical analysis yields a score called canonical-R, which can be interpreted as the simple correlation between the weighted sums of scores from each set of variables, computed with the weights pertaining to the first canonical root. The canonical-R is fairly substantial (.87) and highly significant (p < .001), suggesting that it is not unlikely that the true correlation between the two sets of constructs is very high. The canonical-R^2 indicates that the stickiness canonical

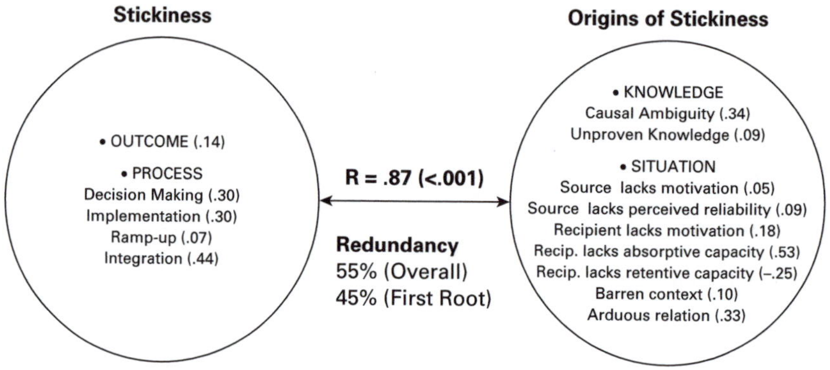

Stickiness   **Origins of Stickiness**

Figure A1.5   *Summary of canonical correlation results*

variate and the origins-of-stickiness canonical variate share about 75 per cent of the variance.

Additional insight about the overall correlation between the two sets of variables is obtained by inspecting the redundancy scores, which measure the redundancy of one set of variables given the other set of variables. The redundancy scores are obtained by multiplying the canonical-R^2 by the proportion of variance extracted, which is computed by summing the squared canonical weights in each canonical variate and dividing by the number of variables in that variate. Hence, there are two redundancy scores, one for the left-side variables and the other for the right-side variables.

The redundancy scores computed with only the first canonical root indicate that, given the stickiness variables, it is possible to account for 29 per cent of the variance on the origins-of-stickiness variables. Conversely, given the origins-of-stickiness variables, it is possible to account for roughly 45 per cent of the variance on the stickiness variables.

Because the canonical roots are uncorrelated, the redundancies can be summed across all roots to arrive at a single index of redundancy (as proposed by Stewart and Love, 1968). The total redundancy values, based on all canonical roots, indicate that on the average it is possible to account for 39.1 per cent of the variance in the origins-of-stickiness variables given the stickiness variables, and 55.5 per cent of the variance of the stickiness variables given the origins-of-stickiness variables. These results suggest a fairly strong overall relationship between the variables of the two sets.

The canonical weights reflect the contribution of each construct to its canonical variate – that is, the linear combination of dependent or independent variables to which it belongs. The weights pertain to the standardized (z-transformed) values and thus could be interpreted in the same way as standardized beta coefficients in a regression analysis. Weights therefore can be compared, and the larger the absolute value of a coefficient, the more important is the contribution of the corresponding variable.

The results suggest that the three most important barriers are the lack of absorptive capacity of the recipient (.54), causal ambiguity (.34) and an arduous relationship between the source and the recipient (.33). Contrary to expectation, the coefficient for the recipient's lack of retentive capacity is negative (−.25).

Robustness of results of the extensive phase

Robustness of the multiple regression results

Further analysis was conducted to confirm the stability of the coefficients. Missing data were handled in four different ways, with missing data deleted pairwise, using mean substitution method, replacing the missing indicators with the indicators' mean, once for independent variables only and again for both dependent and independent variables. Results remain stable also when company dummy variables are included in the four regression equations.

The results reported are based on an analysis in which each questionnaire from source, recipient and third party pertaining to any one transfer is treated as a singular and discrete data point. Thus, each transfer – the unit of analysis – is sampled three times. This raises the problem of non-independence of data. To confirm the stability and robustness of the findings, additional analyses were conducted. First, dummy variables were introduced to control for the affiliation of the respondent, i.e. source, recipient or third party. Second, a single observation was created from the three questionnaires for the same transfer, first by averaging all questionnaires, then by averaging only those with high quality of responses, and finally by discarding all but the best questionnaire for each transfer; (highest quality of response). In all these analyses, the models remain highly significant with adj. $R^2 \geq = .27$, samples sizes ranging from 77 to 98 observations. The analyses revealed that with the exception of a single coefficient (unproven knowledge) in the implementation stickiness column, results are otherwise stable, indicating the absence of major specification errors.

Robustness of the canonical correlation results

A key consideration in the objective interpretation of canonical correlation analysis is weight instability (Lambert and Durand, 1975). When weights are unstable, a statistically significant canonical correlation can occur even though the criterion and predictor sets are not strongly related. To rule out that possibility, each dependent variable was regressed separately on the independent variables. All proved to be highly significant, with $R^2_{adj.}$ ranging from .4 to .51. Weight instability is partly a function of sample size and intercorrelation between variables. The canonical analysis used only 87 observations out of the 271 sample points. Because the high number of missing observations was due primarily to non-response to stickiness-outcome items, a second canonical analysis was conducted in which that variable was excluded from the left-side canonical variate. The number of valid cases was thus raised to 142. This second analysis confirmed that the canonical-R is a robust finding (the canonical-R decreases slightly to .84 and remains highly significant). As expected, variations occur both on the left- and right-side canonical weights, yet the rank ordering of the weights does not change on the left side. On the right side the rank ordering does not change for the three most important variables, which continue to account for most of the variance on their canonical variate. The change in ranking and the fluctuation of the parameters suggest that the sample size may be too small to ensure the stability of any but the three largest canonical weights, yet it does not undermine the overall conclusion derived from the analysis, i.e. that knowledge-related barriers dominate motivation-related barriers.

The negative sign on the canonical weight of the lack of recipient retentive capacity (−.25) is also a stable finding. In interpreting this finding, it is important to note that all transfers in the sample were reported between four and eight months after the first-day recipients started using the transferred knowledge. That is a relatively short time in which to develop effective retentive capacity for the use of new knowledge, let alone to reveal the influence of that capacity on stickiness (Lawless, 1987; Tyre and Orlikowski, 1994). A potential explanation for this finding is that retentive capacity, when measured early in the integration stage, represents to some extent the formalized routine use of *previous* knowledge. Hence, unlearning (Hedberg, 1981) will be required to replace prior knowledge (Hamel, 1991). Dismantling retentive capacity for prior knowledge contributes to stickiness.

The plot of the canonical scores computed with the first root solution did not reveal outliers, a non-linear (U-or S-shaped) trend around the regression line, or clusters of cases. That finding rules out major violations of a main assumption of canonical correlation analysis and suggests that the sample is homogeneous.

Limitations

Any conclusion drawn from this study should be qualified with an explicit acknowledgment of its limitations. First, the extensive reliance on subjective data calls for caution in the interpretation of the results. Second, the sampling suffers from survival bias because, despite best efforts to identify them, problematic or aborted transfers remained elusive. Third, and closely related, none of the transfers reported was aborted during or closely after the gestation period that precedes the actual beginning of the transfer. Thus, the sample of transfers used in the survey does not include any extreme example of difficulty. Finally, the study encompassed only a selected group of companies, and in some cases the number of valid observations was relatively limited.

It should be stressed that the test of the hypothesis in a cross-sectional research design does not provide, in and of itself, a test for causality but only for concomitance or association. Furthermore, it is assumed, as a first approximation, that the origins of stickiness are structural features of the transfer. This assumption needs careful scrutiny because some predictors of stickiness, such as the degree of the motivation of the source or the recipient, may fluctuate as the transfer unfolds. This raises the problem of simultaneity and calls for caution in imputing causal direction to the results.

Notes

1. With over 300 members, the IBC is currently the largest international network of benchmarking firms.

2. There are very few studies of transfer of practices inside firms. Most existing studies are circumscribed to only one firm.

3. In many cases it was not possible to identify a third party to the transfer.

4. The practices studied are not listed fully to preserve confidentiality. Examples of technical practices are Software Development Process and Drafting Standards.

Examples of administrative practices are Activity Based Costing (ABC) and Upward Appraisal.

5. The coordinators from each company provided a detailed account for each questionnaire sent, thus providing an exhaustive non-response follow-up. The most common justification for non-response was the lack of detailed familiarity with the transfer. Other reasons for non-response were 'refused' or 'left the company'.

6. The average duration of the ramp-up process was one-and-a-half months with surprisingly little variation. Thus all transfers were sampled early on in the integration stage. Because the integration stage has been documented to last one-and-a-half to-two years, a band of three-and-a-half months could be considered narrow.

Appendix 2

INTERNATIONAL **BENCHMARKING** CLEARINGHOUSE

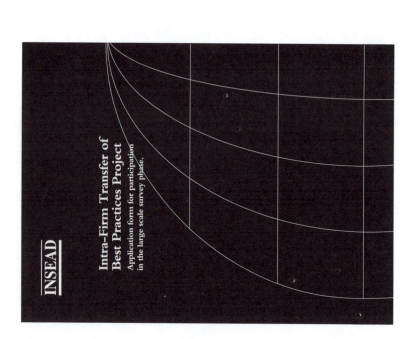

INSEAD

Intra–Firm Transfer of
Best Practices Project

Application form for participation
in the large scale survey phase.

1. THE OPPORTUNITY: PARTICIPATE IN THE LARGE SAMPLE SURVEY

"You can see a high-performance factory or office, but it just doesn't spread. I don't know why."

William Buehler
senior vice president at Xerox
(from Fortune magazine)

Often, you don't have to look too far to find best practice. Internal benchmarking may reveal that the repository of stellar practice, the outstanding center of excellence is simply another unit of your own organization. For example, General Motors has two such excellence centers: the NUMMI plant and the Saturn division. Through a joint venture with Toyota, GM has managed to get the NUMMI car manufacturing plant in Fremont, California, to produce as efficiently as its sister plant, Toyota's in Takaoda, Japan. Similarly, by experimenting with new ways of organizing manufacturing and distribution practices, General Motors has achieved spectacular results in its Saturn division.

Intuitively, one would expect that these better practices will be embraced whole-heartedly by the entire organization. After all, it seems reasonable to expect that a better way of doing things will be recommended by superiors and emulated by peers.

Evidence, however, suggests otherwise. Indeed, GM failed to transfer the practices of the NUMMI plant to the Van-Nuys plant (both in California), and so far, Saturn's success has fostered more resentment from other GM divisions than imitation. Researchers from Harvard Business School have documented the ease of a high-tech firm that experienced severe difficulties in transferring engineering knowledge because the source plants desired to protect proprietary knowledge and because the recipient plants were reluctant to assimilate superior manufacturing technology if that technology was developed at another plant, a disease sometimes diagnosed as the "Not Invented Here," where a technology was either replicated at, or completely relocated to another facility. Far from automatic, the successful transfer of best practices inside the company seems fraught with difficulties.

The objective of the Intra-Firm Transfer of Best Practices project is to identify and understand the sources of difficulty to transfer best practices inside the firm. If the experience of GM evokes uneasy memories of similar experiences within your own organization, if you can clearly identify best practices within your own organization which have not spread satisfactorily and even though you have a hunch you can't really assert why, then you may be interested to participate in the large sample survey phase of the Intra-Firm Transfer of Best Practices Project.

This survey, based on a self administered questionnaire, is the culminating phase of a multi-method, in-depth inquiry into the sources of difficulty to transfer best practices inside the firm. Conscientiously administered, it has the potential to provide you with rigorous, objective evidence of the sources of difficulty to transfer best practices inside your own organization; evidence against which you may test the veracity of existing beliefs and the validity of currently accepted wisdom. You can think of this evidence as a 'map' of the sources of difficulty, a map to assist you in the design and evaluation of organizational mechanisms that will overcome these uncovered sources of difficulty, and thus enable more intense sharing of best practices between sub-units of your own firm. Besides this company specific 'map', the results of the survey will be analyzed statistically and the participating companies will be invited to an exclusive presentation and discussion of the findings and implications of the project.

To be successful, however, the survey requires close collaboration from the participating companies. Unlike most large sample surveys, which focus on the company as a whole, this survey focuses on specific transfer projects inside the company. Because we would like, for each project, to identify the sources of difficulty (which may vary across projects, even within the same company), we'll need to send at least three questionnaires for each one of the project of transfer studied. One questionnaire will be sent to the source of best practice, another to the recipient of best practice, and yet another to the corporate office most directly involved in the particular transfer. Hence, before the questionnaires can be sent, the transfer projects need to be singled out, and three participants from each one of those projects need to be identified. Compiling this information may be as simple as a database query, it may require a somewhat more important team effort, or it may not be doable at all. However, only with this information it will be possible to administer the survey.

For this reason, before we will send the survey to your company, we propose to perform a feasibility test. Feasibility means, first of all, unequivocal top management interest to administer the survey within your

company. If that's the case, we would like a senior executive officer to propose a highly visible and respected person with whom we could coordinate the administration of the survey. We would expect this coordinator to be able and willing to: derive a list of concrete instances of best practice transfer, scrutinize a pilot questionnaire for clarity, and insure that the questionnaires we sent you are returned not only duly completed but also on time.

If you are interested in participating in the survey, we would greatly appreciate if you could express your interest using the attached forms. To express your interest, you'll need to identify a coordinator and build the list of transfer projects. If this seems and turns out to be feasible, then your company may be able to complete successfully the administration of the survey. Otherwise we seriously doubt it. Thus, in the interest of fairness, we will send the survey only to those companies that complete successfully and adequately this first, common sense feasibility test.

We hasten to add that any information exchanged during this project will be treated according to International Benchmarking Clearinghouse's (IBC) Code of Conduct. Specifically, we will treat the information exchange as confidential to our research team and to your company. We will not communicate information to any other party without your prior consent, nor will we communicate externally your company's participation in the study without your prior and explicit permission. We will also keep confidential any contact names. And should we use the information in academic publications, we'll modify it to preserve complete anonymity of participating companies and of individual respondents. Finally, to further facilitate the information exchange, we will have an electronic mailbox in the IBC's on-line Network to assist you throughout the entire process.

The rest of this document contains guidelines to complete the feasibility test, the required forms, and background information on the Intra Firm Transfer of Best Practices Project. We expect to have the forms back by September 30th. Soon after, firms will be notified of the outcome of their application to participate in the survey. On that occasion, the timing for the balance of the project will also be communicated to the admitted companies.

2. WHAT DOES IT TAKE TO PARTICIPATE?

We will send the actual survey to interested companies that have successfully completed the feasibility test. We will evaluate the feasibility test sent to us along three dimensions: 1) the quality of top management support 2) the number and type of practices selected and 3) the number of instances of transfer identified.

FORM 1-top management support: The most important indication of feasibility is the level of interest of top management to administer the survey within the company. Without it, we reckon, little will happen. Quality of top management support is basically determined by two factors: the seniority of the top level executive sponsoring the project and the stature of the coordinator within the organization. Ideally, a very high level executive, such as a Senior Vice President, Corporate Director, a COO, etc., should sponsor the project and nominate the in-company coordinator. An ideal coordinator would have not only a broad, high level perspective of the company, but also the necessary visibility and empowerment to obtain commitment and cooperation from the potential respondents to the survey. Desirably, he or she should also have a direct and intense interest in the data uncovered by the survey. Securing top management support is most important for achieving feasibility.

FORM 2-a list of best practices: With top management support secured, the next step is to select the practices of interest to be studied. Which practices should you select? Perhaps the first requisite is that there exist a consensus within your company that the practice is an important organizational process that merits to be studied. The way the practice is performed should have noticeable impact on the performance of the organization. For example, inadequate customer order processing may impact customer satisfaction and eventually the company's market share.

Besides being important, practices of particular interest are those that seen to have been difficult to transfer. That is, in some cases the transfer was a clear success, in others, a clear failure. Also to identify a study-worthy practice look for evidence of customization of the practice by the recipient. That is, the practice could not be "borrowed" as is, but had to be adapted and fine-tuned by the recipient sub-unit to meet the requirements of its customers, its products, its technology, its regulators, etc. Look also for a practice transferred between units occupying a similar stage in the value chain. Thus, transfer between peer units are the most interesting. One example is a transfer from one sales department to another. Finally, look for a complex practice . Complex means that it cannot comprehended in its entirety in one person's head. Performing this practice requires the coordinated effort of a group of people.

FORM 3-list of transfer projects: For each practice listed in FORM 2 try and identify at least four to five concrete instances of its transfer. Ideally, at least some of these transfers should have been a clear success and some a clear failure. The most relevant type of transfer is inter-unit (eg. inter-divisional, inter-subsidiary, etc). For each instance of transfer identify the source of the practice, the recipient of the practice, and the corporate entity most closely involved with the transfer. In identifying the source, the recipient, and the corporate entity specify the name and location of the unit and also the name of the person that will answer the questionnaire.

The table below summarizes the key criteria for completing successfully the feasibility test: They are meant as a guide, as an ideal to be approached, rather than a strict requirement. The closest these requirements are observed, however, the more likely that your company will meet the feasibility test.

FORM#	ISSUE	KEY CRITERIA
FORM 1	Quality of Top Management Support	Seniority of Sponsor Adequacy of Coordinator
FORM 2	The number and type of practices selected	Important process, difficult to transfer, had to be adapted by the recipient, transferred between peer units, requires the collaborative effort of many individuals
FORM 3	The number of instances of transfer identified.	At least four or five transfers per practice (pref. inter-unit), identity of respondents at source, recipient, and corporate office involved.

Our company ....
wants to participate in the large sample survey phase of the Intra-Firm Transfer of Best Practice Project.

We designate:

NAME ....
POSITION ....

to coordinate the administration of the s

In the spirit of the IBC Code of Conduc
ment made in a timely manner.

Sincerely,

DATE.........................

SIGNATURE ....

NAME ....

POSITION ....

NOTE: Please include the visiting cards of both the appointing senior officer and of the coordinator.

Description: A succinct description of what the practice does.

IBC Process Code: Please indicate in this field the most appropriate code in the IBC process taxonomy for the practice.

Documents Included: If possible, include descriptive documentation on the practice. Use this field to list the documents included

PRACTICE#	DESCRIPTION	IBC PROCESS CODE	DOCUMENTS INCLUDED
1			
2			
3			
4			
5			
6			
2			
8			
3			
11			
12			
13			
14			
15			
16			
17			
18			
19			

#of Practice Transferred: Enter in this field the practice # from Form 2 corresponding to the practice being transferred.
Source: Please identify in this field the source unit, its location, the name of the respondent and his or her position at the time of the transfer.

PRACTICE # of Practice Transferred	SOURCE Unit, Location Respondent Name and Position	RECIPIENT Unit, Location Respondent Name and Position	CORPORATE Department Location Respondent Name and Position	SUCCESS of the TRANSFER Transfer Duration Transfer Cost Performance of received practice	PRACTICE # of Practice Transferred	SOURCE Unit, Location Respondent Name and Position	RECIPIENT Unit, Location Respondent Name and Position	CORPORATE Department Location Respondent Name and Position	SUCCESS of the TRANSFER Transfer Duration Transfer Cost Performance of received practice
1 *Purchasing "cost to Spend" ratio-best practice*	UNIT LOCATION RESPONDENT Name: Position:	UNIT LOCATION RESPONDENT Name: Position:	DEPARTMENT *Corporate Sourcing* LOCATION RESPONDENT Name: Position:	DURATION ☐ more than expected ☐ as expected ☐ less than expected COST ☐ more than expected ☐ as expected ☐ less than expected PERFORMANCE ☐ better than expected ☐ as expected ☐ lower than expected		UNIT LOCATION RESPONDENT Name: Position:	UNIT LOCATION RESPONDENT Name: Position:	DEPARTMENT LOCATION RESPONDENT Name: Position:	PERFORMANCE ☐ better than expected ☐ as expected ☐ lower than expected DURATION ☐ more than expected ☐ as expected ☐ less than expectd COST ...
2 *Purchasing Client Satisfaction Process*	UNIT LOCATION RESPONDENT Name: Position:	UNIT LOCATION RESPONDENT Name: Position:	DEPARTMENT *Same as Above* LOCATION RESPONDENT Name: Position:	PERFORMANCE ☐ better than expected ☐ as expected ☐ lower than expected DURATION ☐ more than expected ☐ as expected ☐ less than expected COST ☐ more than expected		UNIT LOCATION RESPONDENT Name: Position:	UNIT LOCATION RESPONDENT Name: Position:	DEPARTMENT LOCATION RESPONDENT Name: Position:	PERFORMANCE ☐ better than expected ☐ as expected ☐ lower than expected DURATION ☐ more than expected ☐ as expected ☐ less than expected COST ☐ more than expected ☐ as expected ☐ less than expected
3 *Purchasing Supplies Continuous Improvement Process*	UNIT LOCATION RESPONDENT Name: Position:	UNIT LOCATION RESPONDENT Name: Position:	DEPARTMENT *Same as Above* LOCATION RESPONDENT Name: Position:	☐ as expected ☐ less than expected PERFORMANCE ☐ better than expected ☐ as expected ☐ less than expected DURATION ☐ more than expected ☐ as expected ☐ less than expected COST ☐ more than expected ☐ as expected ☐ less than expected ☐ more than expected ☐ as expected ☐ less than expected		UNIT LOCATION RESPONDENT Name: Position:	RESPONDENT Name: Position:	RESPONDENT Name: Position:	☐ more than expected ☐ as expected ☐ less than expected PERFORMANCE ☐ better than expected ☐ as expected ☐ less than expected DURATION ☐ more than expected ☐ as expected ☐ less than expected COST ☐ more than expected ☐ as expected ☐ less than expected PERFORMANCE ☐ better than expected ☐ as expected ☐ lower than expected

Recipient: Please identify in this field the recipient unit, its location, the name of the respondent and his or her position *at the time of the transfer*.

Corporate: Please identify in the field the corporate dept most directly involve with the transfer; its location, the name of the respondent and his or her position *at the time of the transfer*.

Success of the Transfer: For each one of the three categories, ie. TIME, COST, and PERFORMANCE, choose one of the three options that most closely corresponds to reality. Performance refers to the performance of the practice in the recipient unit.

The Intra Firm Transfer of Best Practices Project, started in July 1992, in the context of the dissertation work of Gabriel Szulanski, in partial fulfillment of the requirements for a Ph.D. degree in Strategic Management. In line with practice in most top U.S. schools, this dissertation project is seen at INSEAD as a serious research effort expected to span two years of fully dedicated work and which should help illuminate an important issue for managers with the aim to advance the theory and practice of management. The project purports to study successful and not so successful efforts to transfer best practice to analyze the various factors that influence the process of transfer; to learn how best practice is transferred, and also what helps and what hinders the transfer of best practice inside firms. The research is entirely funded by INSEAD and the ultimate goal of this effort is to develop a fresh theoretical perspective on what helps and what hinders intra-firm transfer of best practice.

The research design consist of three phases. During the first, clinical phase, case studies will be written to document clear instances of success and of failure in transferring best practice within three selected US and European companies. During the second phase, a survey will be administered within these three selected companies to obtain statistically robust and generalizable evidence on the transfer of best practice within those companies. To insure the relevance and the accuracy of the data obtained from the survey, the questionnaire will be finalized and administered once the fieldwork is at an advanced stage. This decision to so time the administration of the questionnaire is based on the belief that questions phrased in familiar language will help the respondents to better relate to the questions and to provide more precise and relevant answers. The learnings gathered during the first two phases of the research will be used to develop a questionnaire for the large sample survey phase, in which you are being invited to participate.

INSEAD AT A GLANCE

INSEAD is an international business school situated on the edge of the forest of Fontainebleau, 65 Kms south of Paris. It was created in 1959 and is Europe's largest postgraduate business school.

The cultural diversity of participants, faculty, corporate partners and the spectrum of activities on campus make INSEAD a unique learning environment. Committed to excellence in both management education and research, INSEAD offers:

The MBA programme

This is a ten-month international programme in general management, admitting currently 460 students a year. A typical MBA class is represented by around 40 nationalities, has an average age of 28 and average professional experience of 4 years.

In 1991/92, about 1400 executives attended from over 1000 corporations.

In addition, company specific programmes are tailor-made for leading international companies to offer them the most suitable programme for their management development needs.

The PHD programme

The recently created Ph.D programme prepares outstanding individuals for careers in the research, study and teaching of management with an international emphasis.

Research and development

Fundamentally, it is through research by the faculty, helped by research associates and Ph.D. students, that INSEAD has been able to acquire knowledge and develop teaching materials.

There are currently 79 faculty members in residence, representing 22 nationalities and about 45 visiting faculty.

The Euro-Asia Center

The Euro-Asia Center is a knowledge, information and communication resource, created to enhance understanding among all communities doing business in Asia. Nearly 100 Asian and Western corporations are members of the Center.

SUMANTRA GHOSHAL

Sumantra Ghoshal is Professor of Management and Digital Equipment Corporation Research Fellow at INSEAD. He holds a doctorate in International Management from MIT and a second doctorate in Business Policy from the Harvard Business School.

His publications include five books and a large number of articles. His latest book, Managing Across Borders: The Transnational solution (co-authored with Professor Christopher A. Bartlett and published by Harvard Business School Press) deals with the orgainzation and management of large world-wide corporations. Based on extensive research in companies such as Unilever, Procter & Gamble, Matsushita, GE, ITT, NEC, KAO and a host of other multinational companies, the book has been translated into many languages including Japanese, Chinese, German, French, Italian and Spanish.

Prior to becoming an academic, Professor Ghoshal had over 13 years of management experience, most of it in various management positions in India's largest corporation. As an academic, he maintains teaching and consulting relationships with a number of European, American and Japanese companies.

GABRIEL SZULANSKI

Gabriel Szulanski is a fourth year Ph.D. student at INSEAD's Ph.D. programme. His dissertation topic is the Transfer of Best Practice inside the Firm. His dissertation work is supervised by Sumantra Ghoshal (chairman), Michael Brimm, Karel O. Cool, and Richard P. Rumelt. He is the recipient of the General Electric fellowship.

Gabriel holds an MBA from Tel Aviv University, with specialization in the Management of Information Systems, a diploma in computer Sciences from the same institution, and a Bachelor of Science in Electrical Engineering from the Technion, Haifa.

Prior to embarking in his doctoral studies, Gabriel had over seven years of full-time working experience as a developer of software and hardware and later as a R&D project manager. He participated in the design, development and implementation of an innovative hotel management system and in the design and implementation of a life support digital communication system, for large police or fire-dept. hq. The system incorporated advanced technologies such as digital audio, distributed multi-processing, and automatic recovery fault tolerance. Later, he managed the development of diagnostic equipment for ISDN digital telephony systems and the development and implementation of a communication network for Israel's National Oil Pipeline.

Correspondence and inquiries about the Intra-Firm Transfer of Best Practice Project should be addressed to:

Gabriel SZULANSKI
INSEAD
Boulevard de Constance
77305 FONTAINEBLEAU - FRANCE
Fax: (33.1) 60.72.42.42
Email: SZULANSK@REFIBA51.BITNETEDU
Or electronic mailbox ' + INSEAD' at IBC on-line network.

BORG has designed this document in full agreement with INSEAD'S INDETITY GUIDELINES

BORG

Concepteur • Editeur

13, rue Sainte Cécile 75009 Paris - FRANCE

Appendix 3: Example of Cover Letter

Thank you for taking part in the Intra-Firm Transfer of Best Practice Survey. With your help we want to learn what helps and what hinders the transfer of best practice inside a firm. [Your company] sees improving its skill in transferring best practice as strategically important and has requested to participate in this survey.

If you'd like to have more detailed information about this study, please contact your company coordinator.

You have received a questionnaire to complete. Each questionnaire focuses on only one transfer of best practice inside your company. The transfer to which the questionnaire relates to is specified in the upper part of the first page of the questionnaire. Your coordinator has identified you as an appropriate respondent for that transfer.

In pilot tests, persons fluent in English successfully completed one questionnaire in less than forty (40) minutes.

Please answer each questionnaire thoroughly. As a representative for that transfer, the quality of your answers will largely determine the usefulness of the findings for the study and for [company]. Thus, the quality of your input is vital. Please, share with us your insights and understanding on what has helped and what has hindered the transfer of the practice inside [company].

You may be assured of complete confidentiality. The questionnaire has an identification code for mailing purposes only. This is so that I may check your name off of the mailing list when your questionnaire is returned. Your name will never be placed in the questionnaire, unless you agree to do so yourself. Also, your responses will be coded by me personally, and all statistical analysis will be at a level of aggregation that will totally prevent identification of individual responses.

Once you have completed all the questionnaire, please return it to [coordinator] as soon as you can. The results from the survey will be communicated to the participating companies on 5 October 1994. To be included in the analysis, completed questionnaires should reach INSEAD before 15 May.

Thanks in advance for sharing your knowledge and wisdom with us.

Sincerely,

Appendix 4: Partial List of Practices Studied

Use of procurement card for purchases of less than $1000
Deployment of strategic plans
Upward appraisal
Activity Based Cost (ABC)
Activity Based Management (ABM)
Creation of new reservation systems
Software development process
Software maintenance
Value engineering
Best practices management
Engineering productivity
Auto strip stock reeling
Connector marking
Selective plating technology
Design review process
Project management
Process capability studies
Statistical process control
Drafting standards
Resident statistical engineering resources
Design of experiments
Boston Square sourcing strategy
Physician-led care coordination rounds process
ER based pre-admission care coordinator process
Emergency prospective review and critical care transport process
Systematic approach to the management of low back pain process
Same-day appointment access process
The Care Team (dedicated) staffing model process
IS implementation process
'Castrol + Plus' service concept
Workshop support marketing
Commercial sales practices
Product formulation concepts
Customer query handling
FSMA revenue breakthrough
Customer software problem management

Appendix 5: Questionnaire Phase II

«Transfer_ID», «Type»

Your Name:
Your Position:

Best Practice Transferred: «practice», «Description»
Source Unit: «source», «srclocation»
Recipient Unit: «recipient», «reclocation»
Third party: «corporate», «corlocation»

1. The Transfer of «Practice»

a) The transfer of «practice» from «source» to «recipient» was: (*circle one option*)

1. MANDATED BY TOP MANAGEMENT
2. STRONGLY ENCOURAGED
3. FAVOURED
4. OPTIONAL
5. ENTIRELY SPONTANEOUS

a) Who, in your opinion, initiated the transfer of «practice» from «source» to «recipient»? (*tick one or more*)

☐ «SOURCE»
☐ «RECIPIENT»
☐ «CORPORATE»
☐ OTHER (PLEASE SPECIFY)
....

b) Why, in your opinion, was the transfer attempted?
....

1.1 CHRONOLOGY

(While answering the questions in this section, you may find it useful to refer back to discussions, reports, visits, presentations, meetings or to your own personal calendar)

a) Approx. when was it decided to proceed with the
transfer of «practice» from «source» to «recipient»?   __ / __ / __
                                                            DY   MN   YR

b) <u>Relative to the initial plan</u>, the start of the transfer was actually:

    1. ADVANCED BY MORE THAN ONE MONTH
    2. ADVANCED BY LESS THAN ONE MONTH
    3. NOT RESCHEDULED
    4. DELAYED BY LESS THAN ONE MONTH
    5. DELAYED BY MORE THAN ONE MONTH

c) Approx. when did «practice» become operational in «recipient»?

    __ / __ / __
    DY   MN   YR

d) Relative to the initial plan, the first day that «practice» became operational in «recipient» was actually: (*circle one option*)

    1. ADVANCED BY MORE THAN ONE MONTH
    2. ADVANCED BY LESS THAN ONE MONTH
    3. NOT RESCHEDULED
    4. DELAYED BY LESS THAN ONE MONTH
    5. DELAYED BY MORE THAN ONE MONTH

e) Approx. when was «recipient» first able to perform «practice» entirely on its own? (i.e. without any assistance from «source» corporate or external consultants)

    __ / __ / __
    DY   MN   YR

f) <u>Compared to the initial plan</u>, support to «recipient» from «source», from corporate or from external consultants to help it get up to speed with the «practice» was: (*circle one option*)

    1. SHORTENED BY MORE THAN ONE MONTH
    2. SHORTENED BY LESS THAN ONE MONTH
    3. AS PROVISIONED
    4. EXTENDED BY LESS THAN ONE MONTH
    5. EXTENDED BY MORE THAN ONE MONTH

g) Approx. when was «practice» first introduced to «company»?

    __ / __ / __
    DY   MN   YR

h) Approx. when did you learn about the existence of «practice»?

    __ / __ / __
    DY   MN   YR

1.2 SYMPTOMS OF DIFFICULTY

a) Approx. how many people were involved in the transfer? .... PEOPLE

b) How much, do you believe, was the cost the transfer of «practice» from «source» to «recipient»? To compute costs add up the cost of <u>people's time</u> devoted to the transfer (in person-days or Full Time Equivalents), the cost of <u>communications</u> and the cost of <u>travel</u>.

COST TO «SOURCE»	+ COST TO «RECIPIENT»	+ OTHER ORG. COST (PLEASE SPECIFY)	= TOTAL COST
.... $	.... $	................$	...................$

c) Transferring the «practice» cost the «source»: (*circle one option*)
1. MUCH (>30%) MORE THAN EXPECTED
2. SLIGHTLY (<30%) MORE THAN EXPECTED
3. AS EXPECTED
4. SLIGHTLY (<30%) LESS THAN EXPECTED
5. MUCH (>30%) LESS THAN EXPECTED

d) Transferring the «practice» cost «recipient»: (*circle one option*)
1. MUCH (>30%) MORE THAN EXPECTED
2. SLIGHTLY (<30%) MORE THAN EXPECTED
3. AS EXPECTED
4. SLIGHTLY (<30%) LESS THAN EXPECTED
5. MUCH (>30%) LESS THAN EXPECTED

e) How much time elapsed from the decision to initiate the transfer until the «practice» was <u>fully operative</u> at «recipient», <u>without any assistance</u>? ....

f) As «recipient» gained experience with the practice it revised its post-transfer performance expect: (*circle one option*)
1. DRAMATICALLY UPWARD
2. SLIGHTLY UPWARD
3. NO CHANGE
4. SLIGHTLY DOWNWARD
5. DRAMATICALLY DOWNWARD

g) With respect to the quality of the «practice», «recipient» was:
1. VERY SATISFIED
2. SOMEWHAT SATISFIED
3. NEITHER SATISFIED NOR DISSATISFIED
4. SOMEWHAT DISSATISFIED
5. VERY DISSATISFIED

h) With respect to the <u>quality of the transfer</u> of «practice», «recipient» was: (*circle one option*)
1. VERY SATISFIED
2. SOMEWHAT SATISFIED
3. NEITHER SATISFIED NOR DISSATISFIED
4. SOMEWHAT DISSATISFIED
5. VERY DISSATISFIED

i) After the transfer, «recipient»'s performance with «practice» was: (*circle one option*)
1. MARKEDLY BETTER THAN THAT OF «SOURCE»
2. SLIGHTLY BETTER THAN THAT OF «SOURCE»
3. ABOUT SAME THAN THAT OF «SOURCE»
4. SLIGHTLY WORSE THAN THAT OF «SOURCE»
5. MARKEDLY WORSE THAN THAT OF «SOURCE»

j) Compared to that of «source», «recipient»'s «practice» is: (*circle one option*)
1. EXACTLY THE SAME
2. ESSENTIALLY THE SAME
3. SLIGHTLY MODIFIED
4. MARKEDLY MODIFIED
5. COMPLETELY DIFFERENT

1.3 DECIDING TO TRANSFER

a) Ranking the performance of «company»'s units on
their results on «practice» was straightforward.   Y! Y O N N!
b) <u>Within «company»</u>, there existed consensus that
«source» has obtained the best results with «practice».   Y! Y O N N!
c) Compared to <u>external</u> benchmarks, «source» has
obtained best-in-class results with «practice».   Y! Y O N N!
d) «source» could easily explain how it obtained superior
results with «practice».   Y! Y O N N!
e) «source» could easily point to the key components
of «practice».   Y! Y O N N!
f) «source» was reluctant to share crucial knowledge
and information relative to «practice».   Y! Y O N N!
g) Distributing responsibility for the transfer between
«source» and «recipient» generated much conflict.   Y! Y O N N!
h) The transfer of «practice» from «source» to
«recipient» was amply justified.   Y! Y O N N!
i) The decision to transfer «practice» from «source» to «recipient» was formalized
in a document which specifies: (*tick zero, one or more*)

- ☐ THE SCOPE OF THE TRANSFER
- ☐ THE TIMING OF THE TRANSFER
- ☐ THE RESPONSIBILITIES OF «SOURCE»
- ☐ THE RESPONSIBILITIES OF «RECIPIENT»
- ☐ THE POST-TRANSFER ENVIRONMENT OF «RECIPIENT»

1.4 IMPLEMENTING THE TRANSFER

a) «recipient» recognized «source»'s expertise
on «practice».   Y! Y O N N!
b) The transfer of «practice» from «source» to
«recipient» disrupted «source» normal operations.   Y! Y O N N!
c) «recipient» could not free personnel from
regular operations so that it could be properly trained.   Y! Y O N N!
d) Communication of transfer-related information
broke down within «recipient».   Y! Y O N N!
e) «recipient» was able to recognize inadequacies in
«source»'s offerings.   Y! Y O N N!
f) «recipient» knew what questions to ask «source».   Y! Y O N N!
g) «recipient» knew how to recognize its
requirements for «practice».   Y! Y O N N!
h) «recipient» performed unnecessary modifications
to the «practice».   Y! Y O N N!
i) «recipient» modified the «practice» in ways contrary
to expert's advice.   Y! Y O N N!
j) «source» turned out to be less knowledgeable of the
«practice» than it appeared before the transfer was decided.   Y! Y O N N!

k) Much of what «recipient» should have done during
the transfer was eventually completed by «source».   **Y!** Y o N **N!**
l) «source» understood «recipient»'s unique situation.   **Y!** Y o N **N!**
m) All aspects of the transfer of «practice» from «source»
to «recipient» were carefully planned.   **Y!** Y o N **N!**
To use the «practice», «recipient»: (*tick zero, one or more*)

☐ BUILT SPECIALIZED EQUIPMENT
☐ INSTALLED NEW SYSTEMS
☐ HIRED NEW STAFF
☐ OBTAINED BLUEPRINTS OF THE «PRACTICE» FROM «SOURCE»
☐ OBTAINED TRAINING MATERIALS FROM «SOURCE»
☐ SENT PERSONNEL TO BE TRAINED AT «SOURCE»
☐ RECEIVED PERSONNEL FROM «SOURCE»

1.5 GETTING UP TO SPEED

a) «recipient» had a detailed action plan for getting up
to speed with the «practice».   **Y!** Y o N **N!**
b) «recipient» had a specific procedure to analyse and
solve problems encountered with the «practice».   **Y!** Y o N **N!**
c) There was a period of time when both the «practice»
and the practice it replaced coexisted within «recipient».   **Y!** Y o N **N!**
d) «recipient» carefully picked the first day of operation
with the «practice».   **Y!** Y o N **N!**
e) Initially «recipient» 'spoon fed' the «practice»
with carefully selected personnel and raw material
until it got up to speed.   **Y!** Y o N **N!**
f) At first «recipient» measured performance more
often than usual, sometimes reacting too briskly to
transient declines in performance.   **Y!** Y o N **N!**
g) Some people left «recipient» after having been
trained for their new role in the «practice», forcing «recipient»
to hire hastily a replacement and train it 'on the fly.   **Y!** Y o N **N!**
h) Some people turned out to be poorly qualified to
perform their new role in the «practice», forcing
«recipient» to hire hastily a replacement and train
it 'on the fly'.   **Y!** Y o N **N!**
i) The «practice» had unsatisfactory side effects which
«recipient» had to correct.   **Y!** Y o N **N!**
j) By altering the «practice», «recipient» created further
problems which had to be solved.   **Y!** Y o N **N!**
k) «recipient»'s environment turned out to be different
from that of «source» forcing «recipient» to make unforeseen
changes to «practice».   **Y!** Y o N **N!**
l) When «recipient» started operating with the «practice»
all required support systems were in place.   **Y!** Y o N **N!**

m) At first, «recipient»'s personnel were confused
by work directives because: (*tick zero, one or more*)

☐ EQUIPMENT WAS INADEQUATE
☐ TRANSLATION OF DOCUMENTS WAS POOR
☐ «SOURCE» HAD DIFFERENT CONVENTIONS THAN «RECIPIENT»
☐ DOCUMENTATION WAS DEFICIENT

n) Problems that emerged while «recipient» was getting started with «practice»
were mostly solved through changes to: (*circle one option*)

1. THE ORGANIZATION ONLY
2. THE ORGANIZATION MOSTLY, TO THE «PRACTICE» IF THERE WAS NO CHOICE
3. BOTH THE ORGANIZATION AND THE «PRACTICE»
4. THE «PRACTICE» MOSTLY, TO THE ORGANIZATION IF THERE WAS NO CHOICE
5. THE «PRACTICE» ONLY

o) Outside experts (from «source», other units, or external consultants) could
answer questions and solve problems about their specialty but did not have an overall perspective on the «practice».   **Y!** Y o N **N!**

p) «recipient» secured the presence of experts for
as long as it was needed.   **Y!** Y o N **N!**

q) Teams put together to help «recipient» to get up to speed
with the «practice» disbanded because their members
had to attend to other pressing tasks.   **Y!** Y o N **N!**

1.6 INTEGRATING «practice» AT «recipient»

a) Within «recipient», approx. what percentage of
people that could be using the «practice» are
actually using it?   .... %

b) «recipient» has not yet solved all problems caused by
the introduction of the «practice», because energy
and resources were siphoned off by daily work pressures.   **Y!** Y o N **N!**

c) Before turning to other tasks, the experts that helped
«recipient» get up to speed, carefully documented
the problems they encountered and how these
problems were solved.   **Y!** Y o N **N!**

d) «recipient» recognized that solutions to some of the
initial problems were temporary in nature and had to
be replaced sooner or later with more stable ones.   **Y!** Y o N **N!**

e) Some of the 'temporary workarounds' devised to
help «recipient» get up to speed became habitual.   **Y!** Y o N **N!**

f) For the «practice» today, the roles are well defined.   **Y!** Y o N **N!**

g) «recipient» personnel are content to play their
roles in «practice».   **Y!** Y o N **N!**

h) The appropriateness of performing the «practice»
«recipient» has been <u>explicitly questioned</u>
in after its introduction.   **Y!** Y o N **N!**

i) «recipient» has reconsidered its decision to
adopt the «practice».   **Y!** Y o N **N!**

j) «recipient»'s expectations created during the
introduction of the «practice» have been met. **Y!** Y O N **N!**
k) Individual values favour performing the «practice». **Y!** Y O N **N!**
l) It is clear why «recipient» needs the «practice». **Y!** Y O N **N!**
m) The justification for performing the «practice»
at «recipient» makes sense. **Y!** Y O N **N!**
n) The activities accompanying the «practice» are difficult. **Y!** Y O N **N!**
o) The activities accompanying the «practice» are: (*circle one option*)

1. OBVIOUSLY FUNCTIONAL
2. SOMEWHAT AGAINST THE GRAIN OF EXISTING WORK PRACTICES
3. ARBITRARY WITHOUT A BASIS IN REALITY

p) After adopting the «practice», «recipient»: (*tick zero, one or more*)

☐ REPLACED IT WITH A NEW CLEARLY SUPERIOR ALTERNATIVE PRACTICE
☐ CHANGED SOME OF ITS PROCEDURES
☐ DISCONTINUED IT ALTOGETHER
☐ INCREASED ITS ORIGINAL SCALE
☐ DISCOVERED LONG RANGE ILL-EFFECTS
☐ REFOCUSED ATTENTION ON OUTSTANDING PROBLEMS PROMPTED BY A CHARGE IN MANAGEMENT
☐ TACKLED OUTSTANDING PROBLEMS WITH NEW PERSONNEL
☐ PLACED NEW DEMANDS ON IT

«SOURCE»

was capable of (*enter X where appropriate*)	saw benefit in (*enter X where appropriate*)	ACTIVITY
☐	☐	measuring its own performance
☐	☐	comparing it with the performance of other units within «company»
☐	☐	understanding its own practices
☐	☐	sharing this understanding with other units
☐	☐	sharing the limits of this understanding with other units
☐	☐	assessing the feasibility of the transfer to «recipient»
☐	☐	communicating with «recipient»
☐	☐	planning the transfer of «practice» to «recipient»
☐	☐	documenting «practice» for transfer
☐	☐	implementing «recipient»'s support systems
☐	☐	training «recipient»'s personnel
☐	☐	helping troubleshoot the «practice» of «recipient»
☐	☐	helping resolve unexpected problems when these appeared
☐	☐	lending skilled personnel
☐	☐	donating skilled personnel

1.7 MOTIVATION OF «source»

a) Supporting the transfer of «practice» to «recipient»
seriously disrupted «source» operations.   **Y!**   Y   O   N   **N!**

1.8 PERCEIVED RELIABILITY OF «source»

a) «source» and «recipient» have similar Key Success Factors.   **Y!**   Y   O   N   **N!**
b) The personnel from «source» and from «recipient»
received similar training.   **Y!**   Y   O   N   **N!**
c) «source»: (*circle one option*)

    1. INVENTED THE «PRACTICE»
    2. WAS THE FIRST UNIT TO HAVE EXPERIENCE WITH THE «PRACTICE» IN «COMPANY» BUT
    THE «PRACTICE» ORIGINATED OUTSIDE «COMPANY»
    3. RECEIVED THE «PRACTICE» FROM ANOTHER UNIT OF «COMPANY»

d) «source» was able to accommodate the needs of
«recipient» into «practice».   **Y!**   Y   O   N   **N!**
e) «source» had an hidden agenda for transferring
«practice» to «recipient».   **Y!**   Y   O   N   **N!**
f) The superior results that «source» obtained with
«practice» were visible to all units of «company».   **Y!**   Y   O   N   **N!**
g) The superior results that «source» obtained with
«practice» remained stable over time.   **Y!**   Y   O   N   **N!**
h) «source» possessed the necessary resources to
support the transfer of «practice» to «recipient».   **Y!**   Y   O   N   **N!**
i) «source» has a history of successful transfers.   **Y!**   Y   O   N   **N!**

1.9 ABOUT THE «practice»

a) When «recipient» encountered the «practice», this was: (*circle one option*)

    1. A GOOD THING THAT «COMPANY» HAD HEARD OF
    2. SOMETHING «COMPANY» HAD SOME EXPERIENCE WITH
    3. SOMETHING «COMPANY» HAD SUBSTANTIAL EXPERIENCE WITH

b) We had solid proof that «practice» was
really helpful.   **Y!**   Y   O   N   **N!**
c) «practice» contributes significantly to the competitive
advantage of «company».   **Y!**   Y   O   N   **N!**
d) For the success of «company», the «practice» is:
(*circle one option*)

    1. CRITICAL
    2. VERY IMPORTANT
    3. FAIRLY IMPORTANT
    4. FAIRLY UNIMPORTANT
    5. NOT IMPORTANT AT ALL

e) Please explain briefly what is «recipient»'s main gain from adopting or adapting the «practice»:

....

1.10 CHARACTERISTICS OF THE «practice»

a) «practice» is still an art rather than a science.	**Y!**	Y	O	N	**N!**
b) The «practice» is fully repeatable.	**Y!**	Y	O	N	**N!**
c) The «practice» is fully predictable.	**Y!**	Y	O	N	**N!**
d) The limits of the «practice» are fully specified.	**Y!**	Y	O	N	**N!**
e) There is a clear customer for the output of the «practice».	**Y!**	Y	O	N	**N!**
f) With the «practice», we know why a given action results in a given outcome.	**Y!**	Y	O	N	**N!**
g) When a problem surfaced with the «practice», the precise reasons for failure could not be articulated even after the event occurred.	**Y!**	Y	O	N	**N!**
h) There is a precise list of the skills, resources and prerequisites necessary for successfully performing the «practice».	**Y!**	Y	O	N	**N!**
i) It is well known how the components of that list interact to produce «practice»'s output.	**Y!**	Y	O	N	**N!**
j) Operating procedures for the «practice» are available.	**Y!**	Y	O	N	**N!**
k) Useful manuals for the «practice» are available.	**Y!**	Y	O	N	**N!**
l) Existing work manuals and operating procedures describe precisely what people working in the «practice» actually do.	**Y!**	Y	O	N	**N!**
m) The «practice» is complex.	**Y!**	Y	O	N	**N!**
n) The «practice» is very different from alternate processes.	**Y!**	Y	O	N	**N!**
o) Introducing «practice» requires a number of new occupational specialties.	**Y!**	Y	O	N	**N!**
p) The «practice» requires a high degree of professionalism.	**Y!**	Y	O	N	**N!**
q) The «practice» is versatile.	**Y!**	Y	O	N	**N!**
r) The «practice» had to be adapted to make it workable at «recipient».	**Y!**	Y	O	N	**N!**

s) A practice could be thought of as composed of separable modules, some essential for its functioning, some not. Each of these modules may be included or may be excluded during a transfer. Thinking about the «practice» as a set of modules, please circle the most correct assertion:

1. ALL MODULES HAVE BEEN TRANSFERRED TO «RECIPIENT»
2. ONLY SELECTED, BUT ALL THE ESSENTIAL MODULES HAVE BEEN TRANSFERRED TO «RECIPIENT»
3. ONLY THE ESSENTIAL MODULES HAVE BEEN TRANSFERRED TO «RECIPIENT»
4. ONLY SELECTED MODULES, SOME ESSENTIAL SOME NOT, HAVE BEEN TRANSFERRED TO «RECIPIENT»
5. NONE OF THE MODULES HAVE BEEN TRANSFERRED TO «RECIPIENT»

t) Some components for the «practice» were replaced by
existing ones at «recipient».   **Y!** Y o N **N!**

1.11 MOTIVATION OF «recipient»

a) Adopting the «practice» caused «recipient» high
replacement costs (e.g., had to discard equipment or
lay off personnel).   **Y!** Y o N **N!**

b) Introducing «practice» to «recipient» significantly
reduced its personnel.   **Y!** Y o N **N!**

c) «recipient»'s personnel reacted to the introduction of «practice» with: (*tick one or more*)

- ☐ ENTHUSIASM
- ☐ COOPERATION
- ☐ TOLERANCE
- ☐ PASSIVITY
- ☐ FOOT DRAGGING
- ☐ FEIGNED ACCEPTANCE
- ☐ HIDDEN SABOTAGE
- ☐ OUTRIGHT REJECTION
- ☐ OTHER (*please specify*) ....

d) «recipient»'s requirements were unique and therefore
unlikely to be satisfied by «source»'s «practice».   **Y!** Y o N **N!**

«RECIPIENT»		
was capable of (*enter X where appropriate*)	saw benefit in (*enter X where appropriate*)	ACTIVITY
☐	☐	measuring its own performance
☐	☐	comparing it with that of other units
☐	☐	understanding its own practices
☐	☐	absorbing «source»'s understanding
☐	☐	analysing the feasibility of adopting «practice»
☐	☐	communicating its needs to «source»
☐	☐	planning the transfer
☐	☐	implementing the systems and facilities for «practice»
☐	☐	assigning personnel full time to the transfer
☐	☐	assigning personnel to be trained in «practice»
☐	☐	understanding the implications of the transfer
☐	☐	troubleshooting «practice» on its own
☐	☐	ensuring that its people knew their jobs
☐	☐	ensuring that its people consented to keep doing their jobs

e) By embracing «source»'s «practice», «recipient»
lost status within «company». **Y!** Y o N **N!**
f) By embracing «source»'s «practice», «recipient»
exposed its weaknesses. **Y!** Y o N **N!**
g) The transfer increased outside interference to
«recipient»'s operation. **Y!** Y o N **N!**
h) By visiting «source», «recipient» got comfortable
that the «practice» worked. **Y!** Y o N **N!**

1.12 LEARNING CAPACITY OF «recipient»

a) «recipient» had never done something like
the «practice». **Y!** Y o N **N!**
b) Members of «recipient» have a common language
to deal with the «practice». **Y!** Y o N **N!**
c) «recipient» had a vision of what it was trying to
achieve through the transfer. **Y!** Y o N **N!**
d) «recipient» had information on the state-of-the-art
of the «practice». **Y!** Y o N **N!**
e) «recipient» had a clear division of roles and
responsibilities to implement the «practice». **Y!** Y o N **N!**
f) «recipient» had the necessary skills to implement
the «practice». **Y!** Y o N **N!**
g) In the past, «recipient» adopted other practices. **Y!** Y o N **N!**
h) In the past, «recipient» adopted similar practices
to the «practice». **Y!** Y o N **N!**
i) «recipient» had the technical competence to absorb
the «practice». **Y!** Y o N **N!**
j) «recipient» had the managerial competence to absorb
the «practice». **Y!** Y o N **N!**
k) When new information related to the «practice»
becomes available, it is well known who can best exploit
it within «recipient». **Y!** Y o N **N!**
l) It is well known who can help solve problems
associated with the «practice». **Y!** Y o N **N!**

1.13 RETENTIVE CAPACITY OF «recipient»

a) «recipient» periodically retrains existing personnel
on the «practice». **Y!** Y o N **N!**
b) To train new personnel on the «practice», «recipient»: (*tick zero, one or more*)

☐ TRAINS ON THE JOB
☐ ASSIGNS A PERSONAL TUTOR
☐ PROVIDES FORMAL TRAINING

c) «recipient» has mechanisms to detect malfunctions of
the «practice». **Y!** Y o N **N!**

d) «recipient» regularly measures performance
and corrects problems as soon as these happen. **Y!** Y O N **N!**
e) «recipient»'s personnel can predict how they will
be rewarded for good performance in the «practice». **Y!** Y O N **N!**
f) «recipient»'s personnel are provided with numerous
opportunities to commit freely and publicly to perform
their role in the «practice». **Y!** Y O N **N!**
g) At «recipient» there is a clear focal point for the
«practice». **Y!** Y O N **N!**
h) Experience with the «practice» expands career
opportunities within «company». **Y!** Y O N **N!**
i) It is clear why the «practice» is necessary for «recipient». **Y!** Y O N **N!**

1.14 «company»

a) Existing performance measures of the «practice» are
detailed enough to be meaningful. **Y!** Y O N **N!**
b) Performance measures of the «practice» are taken
frequently enough to be timely. **Y!** Y O N **N!**
c) Performance measures of the «practice» from different
units are easily comparable. **Y!** Y O N **N!**
d) «company» enforces company-wide standard policies
with respect to the «practice». **Y!** Y O N **N!**
e) The success of best-in-class units in the «practice»
is made visible through rewards (e.g., internal publicity,
external publicity, presidential awards). **Y!** Y O N **N!**
f) Facilitating the transfer of the «practice» between
units is a corporate priority. **Y!** Y O N **N!**
g) Opting out of common approaches is encouraged
at «company». **Y!** Y O N **N!**
h) At «company» there is constant pressure to improve
performance. **Y!** Y O N **N!**
i) Regardless of expense, communication between
units is encouraged at «company». **Y!** Y O N **N!**
j) It is easy to justify time spent visiting other units. **Y!** Y O N **N!**
k) To visit another unit, it is easy to justify travel expenses. **Y!** Y O N **N!**
l) Overt comparison of results by units is: (*circle one option*)

   1. ENFORCED
   2. EXPECTED
   3. ENCOURAGED
   4. NEITHER ENCOURAGED NOR DISCOURAGED
   5. DISCOURAGED
   6. NOT EXPECTED
   7. FORBIDDEN

m) At «company», improving performance by copying
and adapting practices from other units is as legitimate
as improving performance by devising original solutions. **Y!** Y O N **N!**

n) At «company», a unit that exposes those needs that it
is unable to meet on its own loses status.   **Y!**   Y   O   N   **N!**

o) At «company», a unit that exposes unresolved problems
loses status.   **Y!**   Y   O   N   **N!**

p) At «company», units fiercely compete with each other.   **Y!**   Y   O   N   **N!**

q) At «company», despite structural differences
units can always learn from one another.   **Y!**   Y   O   N   **N!**

r) At «company», it is usual practice to relocate
skilled personnel.   **Y!**   Y   O   N   **N!**

s) Normally a best-in-class practice is most likely to be
found outside «company».   **Y!**   Y   O   N   **N!**

t) At «company», managers seem to prefer to use
external sources of help and support even though they
are more expensive and less helpful.   **Y!**   Y   O   N   **N!**

u) At «company», corporate pride and values encourage
managers not to look outside for help or to share with
the outside.   **Y!**   Y   O   N   **N!**

2. TRANSFER MECHANISMS

In answering the questions in this section, please refer to the list of mechanisms in the last page of the questionnaire. In answering the questions, you may simply enter numbers from that list. Also, in answering the questions please specify whether other parties besides the source and the recipient of the best practice, such as corporate or outside consultants, were involved in implementing the mechanisms.

Please list what is normally done to <u>identify units that excel</u> at «practice» within «company».

....
....

Please list what units that excel at «practice» normally do to <u>share how</u> they achieve superior results.

....
....

Please list what is normally done <u>to discover unmet needs</u> within «company».

....
....

Please list what is normally done <u>to examine the feasibility of a transfer</u> of «practice» within «company».

....
....

Please list in what ways «source» and «recipient» usually <u>communicate</u>.

....
....

Please list what is normally done <u>to plan the logistics of a transfer</u> of «practice» within «company».

....
....

Please list what is normally done within «company» <u>to develop the infrastructure to support</u> the «practice».

....
....

Please list what is normally done <u>to train</u> on «practice» within «company».

....
....

Please list what is normally done to help a new adopter of «practice» <u>get up to speed</u>.

....
....

Please list what is normally done to insure that the «practice» <u>integrates smoothly</u> with other existing practices.

....
....

3. BACKGROUND INFORMATION

3.1 *About your unit*

a) Approx. how many people worked in your unit at the
time the transfer begun?   .... PEOPLE
b) When the transfer of «practice» begun, the number of
people working in your unit was: (*circle one option*)

1. RAPIDLY INCREASING
2. SLOWLY INCREASING
3. STABLE
4. SLOWLY DECREASING
5. RAPIDLY DECREASING

c) When the transfer of «practice» begun, «company» was: (*circle one option*)

1. STRUGGLING TO SURVIVE
2. HAVING DIFFICULTIES
3. DOING FINE
4. DOING GREAT

d) Compared to similar units within «company», in terms of business performance your unit ranks: (*circle one option*)

1. BEST
2. SUPERIOR
3. AVERAGE
4. INFERIOR
5. WORST

e) Approx. in which year was your unit established ? _ _ _ _

3.2 *The relationship between «source» and «recipient»*

a) On average, «source» contacts «recipient»: (*circle one option*)

1. DAILY
2. WEEKLY
3. MONTHLY
4. YEARLY
5. LESS THAN YEARLY

b) On average, «recipient» contacts «source»: (*circle one option*)

1. DAILY
2. WEEKLY
3. MONTHLY
4. YEARLY
5. LESS THAN YEARLY

c) «recipient» relationship with «source» is: .... years old.

d) Communication between «source» and «recipient» is: (*circle one option*)

1. VERY EASY
2. FAIRLY EASY
3. FAIRLY DEMANDING
4. VERY DEMANDING

e) Collaboration between «source» and «recipient»: (*circle one option*)

1. IS SOUGHT ACTIVELY BY «SOURCE»
2. IS WELL RECEIVED BUT NOT SOUGHT BY «SOURCE»
3. IS PREFERABLY AVOIDED BY «SOURCE»
4. OCCURS ONLY IF «SOURCE» HAS NO CHOICE

f) Collaboration between «source» and «recipient»: (*circle one option*)

1. IS SOUGHT ACTIVELY BY «RECIPIENT»
2. IS WELL RECEIVED BUT NOT SOUGHT BY «RECIPIENT»
3. IS PREFERABLY AVOIDED BY «RECIPIENT»
4. OCCURS ONLY IF «RECIPIENT» HAS NO CHOICE

g) «source» depends on «recipient» for its day-to-day
operations.   **Y!** Y O N **N!**

h) «recipient» depends on «source» for its
day-to-day operations.   **Y!** Y O N **N!**

4. YOUR WISDOM

Reflecting back on the transfer of «practice» between «source» and «recipient», what was the single most important difficulty experienced during that transfer?

....
....

Reflecting back on the transfer of «practice» between «source» and «recipient». What would have been the single most important action to facilitate that transfer?

....
....

«Q1»

....
....

«Q2»

....
....

«Q3»

....
....

5. THANK YOU!

Thank you very much for your time and effort and for sharing your knowledge and experience. If you have any other information, ideas, or comments you would like to share, please attach a separate statement to this questionnaire.

Should you have any questions regarding the questionnaire, please contact your coordinator, «coordinatorfirst» «coordinatorlast» at «phone».

6. LIST OF MECHANISMS

The mechanisms listed below are commonly cited facilitators of best practice transfer. You may want to refer to this list while answering section 2 and section 4.

1 audit teams
2 central advisor/expert
3 central function controlling activity
4 company video films
5 conferences
6 conventions
7 corporate sets policy based on best unit

8 formal control procedures
9 informal control procedures
10 intra-company forums
11 line instruction
12 multi-unit task teams
13 operational reviews
14 organized periodic short (less than a week) visits

15 project team develops recommendations
16 project team surveys current practice and develops standards for best practice.
17 re-engineering efforts
18 skill pool management
19 total quality management efforts
20 best practice manuals
21 central consulting resource
22 company newsletters
23 company-wide database of best practices
24 continuous improvement efforts
25 corporate monitors units and decides what is best practice
26 discussions held to influence units to raise their quality
27 help from other units

28 informal visits
29 lead business units
30 meet in a conference and agree to help each other
31 newsletter describing new methods being developed by a unit
32 organized periodic long (more than one week) visits
33 presentations
34 project team recommends guidelines
35 project teams other
36 rotation of personnel
37 startup team
38 workshops

References

Adler, P.S. (1990) 'Shared learning'. *Management Science* 36 (8): 938–57.

Allen, M. and Stiff, J. (1989) 'Testing three models for the sleeper effect'. *Western Journal of Speech Communication* 53: 411–26.

Amit, R. and Schoemaker, P.J.H. (1993) 'Strategic assets and organizational rent'. *Strategic Management Journal* 14 (1): 33–46.

Argote, L. (1999) *Organizational Learning: Creating, Retaining, and Transferring Knowledge*. Boston: Kluwer Academic.

Argote, L., Beckman, S.L. and Epple, D. (1990) 'The persistence and transfer of learning in industrial settings'. *Management Science* 36 (2): 140–54.

Argyris, C. and Schon, D.A. (1978) *Organizational Learning*. Reading, MA: Addison-Wesley.

Armor, D.J. (1974) 'Theta reliability and factor scaling'. In *Sociological Methodology 1973–1974*, edited by H.L. Costner. San Francisco: Jossey-Bass, pp. 17–50.

Arrow, K.J. (1962) 'The economic implications of learning by doing'. *Review of Economic Studies* 29: 155–73.

Arrow, K.J. (1962) 'Economic welfare and the allocation of resources for invention'. In *The Rate and Direction of Inventive Activity*, edited by R.R. Nelson. Princeton: Princeton University Press, pp. 609–25.

Arrow, K.J. (1974) *The Limits of Organization*. New York: Norton.

Attewell, P. (1992) 'Technology diffusion and organizational learning: the case of business computing'. *Organization Science* 3 (1): 1–19.

Babakus, E., Ferguson Jr., C.E. and Joereskog, K.G. (1987) 'The sensitivity of confirmatory maximum likelihood factor analysis to violations of measurement scale and distributional assumptions'. *Journal of Marketing Research* 24 (May): 222–8.

Bain, J.S. (1956) *Barriers to New Competition*. Cambridge, MA: Harvard University Press.

Balm, G.J. (1992) *Benchmarking: A Practitioner's Guide for Becoming and Staying Best of the Best*. Schaumburg, IL: QPMA Press.

Baloff, N. (1970) 'Startup management'. *IEEE Transactions on Engineering Management* EM-17 (4), November: 132–41.

Barber, B. (1983) *The Logic and Limit of Trust*. New Brunswick, NJ: Rutgers University Press.

Barley, S.R. (1990) 'Images of imaging: notes on doing longitudinal fieldwork'. *Organization Science* 1 (3): 220–47.

Barney, J.B. (1986) 'Strategic factor markets: expectations, luck and business strategy'. *Management Science* 32 (10): 1231–41.

Bartlett, C.A. and Ghoshal, S. (1989) *Managing Across Borders: The Transnational Solution*. Boston, MA: Hutchinson Business Books.

Bartlett, C.A. and Ghoshal, S. (1993) 'Beyond the M-form: toward a managerial theory of the firm'. *Strategic Management Journal* 14 (Winter Special Issue): 23–46.

Belliveau, M., O'Reilly, C. and Wade, J. (1996) 'Social capital at the top: effects of social similarity and status on CEO compensation.' *Academy of Management Journal* 39 (6): 1568–93.

Benjamin, B. and Podolny, J. (1999) 'Status, quality and social order in the California wine industry'. *Administrative Science Quarterly* 44 (3): 563–89.

Berber, B. (1983) *The Logic and Limits of Trust*.

Berger, P.L. and Luckman, T. (1966) *The Social Construction of Reality: A Treatise in the Sociology of Knowledge*. Garden City, NY: Doubleday.

Bohn, R.E. (1994) 'Measuring and managing technological knowledge'. *Sloan Management Review* Fall: 61–73.

Boland, R.J., Jr. and Tenkasi, R.V. (1995) 'Perspective making and perspective taking in communities of knowing'. *Organization Science* 6 (4): 350–72.

Bower, J.L. (1970) *Managing the Resource Allocation Process*. Boston, MA: Harvard Business School Press.

Brooks, F.P. (1995) *The Mythical Man-Month: Essays on Software Engineering*. Reading, MA: Addison-Wesley.

Brown, C. and Reich, M. (1989) 'When does union–management cooperation work? A look at NUMMI and GM-Van Nuys'. *California Management Review* 31 (4): 26–44.

Brown, J.S. and Duguid, P. (1991) 'Organizational learning and communities-of-practice: toward a unified view of working, learning, and innovation'. *Organization Science* 2 (1): 40–57.

Buttolph, D. (1992) 'A new look at adaptation'. *Knowledge: Creation, Diffusion, Utilization* 13 (4): 460–70.

Cairncross, F. (2000) 'Inside the Machine'. *The Economist,* November: 38–9.

Camp, R.C. (1989) *Benchmarking: The Search for Industry Best Practices that Lead to Superior Performance*. Milwaukee, WN: ASQC Quality Press.

Capon, N. and Hulbert, J. (1973) 'The sleeper effect: an awakening'. *Public Opinion Quarterly* 37 (3): 333–58.

Carley, K. (1991) 'A theory of group stability'. *American Sociological Review* 56 (3): 331–54.

Carlile, P.R. (2002) 'A pragmatic view of knowledge and boundaries: boundary objects in new product development'. *Organization Science*.

Carmines, E.G. and Zeller, R.A. (1979) *Reliability and Validity Assessment*. Beverly Hills, CA: Sage.

Caves, R. and Porter, M. (1977) 'From entry barriers to mobility barriers'. *Quarterly Journal of Economics* 91: 241–61.

Chakravarthy, B.S. and Doz, Y. (1992) 'Strategy process research: focusing on corporate self-renewal'. *Strategic Management Journal* 13 (Summer): 5–15.

Chew, W.B. (1991) *Productivity, Investment and Murphy's Law*. Boston, MA: Harvard Business School.

Chew, W.B., Bresnahan, T.F. and Clark, K.B. (1990) 'Measurement, coordination, and learning in a multiplant network'. In *Measures for Manufacturing Excellence*, edited by R.S. Kaplan. Boston, MA: Harvard Business School, pp. 129–62.

Chi, T. (1994) 'Trading in strategic resources: necessary conditions, transaction cost problems, and choice of exchange structure'. *Strategic Management Journal* 15 (4): 271–90.

Cohen, W.M. and Levinthal, D. (1989) 'Innovation and learning: the two faces of R&D'. *The Economic Journal* 99: 569–96.

Cohen, W.M. and Levinthal, D. (1990) 'Absorptive capacity: a new perspective on learning and innovation'. *Administrative Science Quarterly* 35 (1): 128–52.

Conner, K.R. (1991) 'An historical comparison of resource-based theory and five schools of thought within industrial organization economics: Do we have a new theory of the firm?' *Journal of Management* (17): 121–54.

Cox, E.P.I. (1980) 'The optimal number of response alternatives for a scale: a review'. *Journal of Marketing Research* 17 (November): 407–22.

Crosby, P.B. (1984) *Quality Without Tears.* New York: McGraw-Hill.

Curall, S. and Judge, T. (1995) 'Measuring trust between organizational boundary role persons'. *Organizational Behavior and Human Decision Processes* 64: 151–70.

Cyert, R.M. and March, J.G. (1963) *A Behavioral Theory of the Firm.* Englewood Cliffs, NJ: Prentice-Hall.

Darr, E.D., Argote, L. and Epple, D. (1995) 'The acquisition, transfer and depreciation of knowledge in service organizations: productivity in franchises'. *Management Science* 41 (11): 1750–63.

Deutsch, G.M. (2000) *Rank Xerox Team C: Global Transfer of Best Practices.* Philadelphia, PA: Wharton.

Dewar, R.D. and Dutton, J.E. (1986) 'The adoption of radical and incremental innovations: an empirical analysis'. *Management Science* 32 (11): 1422–33.

Dierickx, I. and Cool, K. (1994) 'Competitive strategy, asset accumulation and firm performance'. In *Strategic Groups, Strategic Moves and Performance*, edited by H. Daems and H. Thomas. Oxford: Oxford University Press.

Dillman, D.A. (1978) *'Mail and Telephone Surveys: The Total Design Method.* New York: John Wiley and Sons.

Dosi, G., Nelson, R.R. and Winter, S.G. (eds) (2000) *The Nature and Dynamics of Organizational Capabilities.* Oxford: Oxford University Press.

Doz, Y. (1994) 'Managing core competency for corporate renewal: Towards a managerial theory of core competencies'. INSEAD. Working paper 94/23/SM. May 17.

Doz, Y.L. and Hamel, G. (1998) *Alliance Advantage: The Art of Creating Value Through Partnering.* Boston, MA: Harvard Business School.

Druckman, D. and Bjork, R.A. (eds) (1991) *In the Mind's Eye: Enhancing Human Performance.* Washington, DC: National Academy Press.

Dyer, J.H. (2000) *Relation-specific Capabilities, Barriers to Knowledge Transfers,* and Competitive Advantage. Provo, UT: Marriott School, Brigham Young University.

Eisenhardt, K. (1989) 'Theory building from case study research'. *Academy of Management Review* 14: 532–50.

Eisenhardt, K.M. and Santos, F.M. (2001) 'Knowledge-based view: a new theory of strategy?' In *Handbook of Strategy and Management*, edited by A. Pettigrew, H. Thomas and R. Whittington. London: Sage, pp. 139–164.

Financial Times (1997) 'Xerox makes copies'. *Financial Times*, 13 July.

Foss, N.J., Knudsen, C. and Montgomery, C.A. (1995) 'An exploration of common ground: integrating evolutionary and strategic theories of the firm'. In *Resource-Based and Evolutionary Theories of the Firm*, edited by C.A. Montgomery. London: Kluwer Academic Publishers, pp. 1–17.

Frantz, R.S. (1988) *X-Efficiency: Theory, Evidence and Applications.* Dordrecht: Kluwer.

Freeman, J. (1986) 'Data quality and the development of organizational social science: an editorial essay'. *Administrative Science Quarterly* 31: 298–303.

Galbraith, C.S. (1990) 'Transferring core manufacturing technologies in high tech firms'. *California Management Review* 32 (4): 56–70.

Garud, R. and Nayyar, P.R. (1994) 'Transformantive capacity: continual structuring by intertemporal technology transfer'. *Strategic Management Journal* 15 (5): 365–85.

Gerbing, D.W. and Anderson, J.C. (1988) 'An updated paradigm for scale development incorporating unidimensionality and its assessment'. *Journal of Marketing Research* 25 (May): 186–92.

Ghemawat, P. (1991) *Commitment*. New York: Free Press.

Ghoshal, S. and Bartlett, C.A. (1994) 'Linking organizational context and managerial action: the dimensions of quality of management'. *Strategic Management Journal* 15 (Special Issue, Summer): 91–112.

Gilbert, R.J. (1989) 'Mobility barriers and the value of incumbency'. *Handbook of Industrial Organization* 1: 1059–107.

Gilovich, T. (1991) *How We Know What Isn't So: The Fallibility of Human Reason in Everyday Life*. New York: Free Press.

Glaser, B.L. and Strauss, A.L. (1968) *The Discovery of Grounded Theory: Strategies for Qualitative Research*. Chicago: Aldine.

Glaser, E.M., Abelson, H.H. and Garrison, K.N. (1983) *Putting Knowledge to Use*. San Francisco: Jossey-Bass.

Goodman, P.S. and Associates (1982) *Change in Organizations*. London: Jossey-Bass.

Goodman, P.S., Bazerman, M. and Conlon, E. (1980) 'Institutionalization of planned organizational change'. In *Research in Organizational Behavior*, edited by B.M. Staw and L.L. Cummings. Greenwich, CT: JAI Press, pp. 215–46.

Goold, M., Campbell, A. and Alexander, M. (1994) *Corporate-Level Strategy: Creating Value in the Multibusiness Company*. New York: John Wiley and Sons.

Grant, R.M. (1996) 'Toward a knowledge-based theory of the firm'. *Strategic Management Journal* 17: 109–22.

Groves, R.M. (1987) 'Research on survey data quality'. *Public Opinion Quarterly* 51: S156–S172.

Gupta, A. and Govindarajan, V. (2000) 'Knowledge flows within multinational corporations'. *Strategic Management Journal* 21: 473–96.

Hamel, G. (1991) 'Competition for competence and inter-partner learning within international strategic alliances'. *Strategic Management Journal* 12: 83–103.

Hamel, G. and Prahalad, C.K. (1988) *When Competitors Collaborate*. London: London Business School.

Hammer, M. and Champy, J. (1993) *Reengineering the Corporation: A Manifesto for Business Revolution*. New York: HarperCollins.

Hansen, G.S. and Wernerfelt, B. (1989) 'Determinants of firm performance: the relative importance of economic and organizational factors'. *Strategic Management Journal* 10: 399–411.

Hansen, M. (1999) 'The search-transfer problem: the role of weak ties in sharing knowledge across organization subunits'. *Administrative Science Quarterly* 44: 82–111.

Haspeslagh, P.C. and Jemison, D.B. (1991) *Managing Acquisitions: Creating Value through Corporate Renewal*. New York: Free Press.

Hayes, R.H. and Clark, K.B. (1985) *Exploring the Sources of Productivity Differences at the Factory Level*. New York: John Wiley and Sons.

Hedberg, B. (1981) *How Organizations Learn and Unlearn*. New York: Oxford University Press.

Henderson, R. and Cockburn, I. (1994) 'Measuring competence? Exploring firm effects in pharmaceutical research'. *Strategic Management Journal* 15 (Special Issue, Winter): 63–84.

Henderson, R.M. and Clark, K.B. (1990) 'Architectural innovation: the reconfiguration of existing product technologies and the failure of established firms'. *Administrative Science Quarterly* 35: 9–30.

Hill, C.W.L. (1992) 'Strategies for exploiting technological innovations: when and when not to license'. *Organization Science* 3 (3): 428–41.

Hoopes, D.G. and Postrel, S. (1999) 'Shared knowledge, "glitches", and product development performance'. *Strategic Management Journal* 20 (9): 837–65.

Hounshell, D.A. (1984) *From the American System to Mass Production 1800–1932.* Baltimore, MA: Johns Hopkins University Press.

Hovland, C. and Weiss, W. (1951) 'The influence of source credibility on communication effectiveness'. *Public Opinion Quarterly* 15 (4): 635–50.

Hovland, C., Lumsdaine, A. and Sheffield, F. (1949) *Experiments in Mass Communication.* New York: Wiley.

Howell, R.D. (1987) 'Covariance structure modeling and measurement issues: a note on "interrelations among a channel entity's power sources"'. *Journal of Marketing Research* 24 (February): 119–26.

Huber, G.P. (1991) 'Organizational learning: the contributing processes and the literatures'. *Organization Science* 2 (1): 88–115.

Ishikawa, K. (1985) *What is Total Quality Control?* Englewood Cliffs: NJ: Prentice-Hall.

Jacob, R. (1992) 'Looking ahead in search for the organization of tomorrow'. *Fortune,* 18 May: 66–72.

Jensen, M. and Meckling, W. (1992) 'Specific and general knowledge, and organizational structure'. In *Contract Economics,* edited by . L. Werin and H. Wijkander. Oxford: Blackwell. pp. 251–74.

Jick, T.D. (1979) 'Process and impacts of a merger: Individual and organisational perspectives'. *Administrative Science Quarterly* 24 (4): 602–11.

Juran, J.M. (1988) *Juran's Quality Control Handbook.* New York: McGraw-Hill.

Kaplan, R.S. (1990) *Measures for Manufacturing Excellence.* Boston, MA: Harvard Business School.

Katz, D. and Kahn, R.L. (1982) *The Social Psychology of Organizations.* New York: John Wiley and Sons.

Kelman, H. and Hovland, C. (1953) 'Reinstatement of the communication in delayed measurement of opinion change'. *Journal of Abnormal and Social Psychology* 45: 327–35.

Kerwin, K. and Woodruff, D. (1992) 'Can Olds hitch its wagon to saturn's star?' *Business Week* 23 November: 74.

Kirk, J. and Miller, M.L. (1986) *Reliability and Validity in Qualitative Research.* London: Sage.

Klein, B., Crawford, R.G. and Alchian, A.A. (1978) 'Vertical integration, appropriable rents, and the competitive contracting process'. *Journal of Law and Economics* 21 (2): 297–326.

Knight, F. (1921) *Risk, Uncertainty and Profit.* New York: Houghton Mifflin Co.

Kogut, B. and Zander, U. (1992) 'Knowledge of the firm, combinative capabilities and the replication of technology'. *Organization Science* 3 (3): 383–97.

Kostova, T. (1999) 'Transnational transfer of strategic organizational practices: a contextual perspective'. *Academy of Management Review* 24: 308–24.

Lambert, Z.V. and Durand, R.M. (1975) 'Some precautions in using canonical analysis'. *Journal of Marketing Research* 12 (November): 468–75.

Lawless, M.W. (1987) 'Institutionalization of a management science innovation in police departments'. *Management Science* 33 (2): 244–52.

Leibenstein, H. (1966) 'Allocative efficiency vs. X-efficiency'. *American Economic Review* 56 (June): 392–415.

Lenox, M.J. (1999) *Agency and Information Costs in the Intra-firm Diffusion of Practice*. Boston: Massachusetts Institute of Technology.

Leonard-Barton, D. (1990a) 'A dual methodology for case studies: synergistic use of a longitudinal single site with replicated multiple sites'. *Organization Science* 1 (3): 248–66.

Leonard-Barton, D. (1990b) *Modes of Technology Transfer within Organizations: Point-to-Point versus Diffusion*. Boston: Harvard Business School.

Levin, R.C., Klevorick, A.K. Nelson, R.R. and Winter, S.G. (1987) 'Appropriating the returns from industrial research and development'. *Brookings Papers of Economic Activity* 3: 783–820, 821–31.

Levinthal, D.A. and March, J.G. (1993) 'The myopia of learning'. *Strategic Management Journal* 14 (Special Issue, Winter): 95–112.

Levitt, B. and March, J.G. (1988) 'Organizational learning'. *Annual Review of Sociology* 14: 319–40.

Lewis, J. and Weigert, A. (1985) 'Trust as a social reality'. *Social Forces* 63: 967–85.

Lippman, S.A. and Rumelt, R.P. (1982) 'Uncertain imitability: an analysis of interfirm differences in efficiency under competition'. *Bell Journal of Economics* 13: 418–38.

Main, J. (1992) 'How to steal the best ideas around'. *Fortune* 19 October: 86–9.

Mansfield, E., Romeo, A. Schwartz, M., Teece, D., Wagner, S. and Brach, P. (1983) 'New findings in technology transfer, productivity and development'. *Research Management* March–April: 11–20.

March, J. and Simon, H. (1958) *Organizations*. New York: Wiley.

Marsden, P. V. (1990) 'Network data and measurement'. *Annual Review of Sociology* 16: 435–63.

McAllister, D. (1995) 'Affect- and cognition-based trust as foundation for interpersonal cooperation in organizations'. *Academy of Management Journal* 38 (1): 24–60.

McGahan, A.M. and Porter, M.E. (1997) 'How much does industry matter, really?' *Strategic Management Review* 18 (Special Issue): 15–30.

McGrath, J.E. (1982) 'Dilemmatics, the study of research choices and dilemmas'. In *Judgement Calls in Research*, edited by J.E. McGrath, J. Martin and K.R. Kulka. Beverly Hills, CA: Sage, pp. 69–102.

McIver, J.P. and Carmines, E.G. (1981) *Unidimensional Scaling*. Beverly Hills, CA: Sage.

Mohr, L.B. (1982) *Explaining Organizational Behavior*. San Francisco: Jossey-Bass.

Morrison, D.F. (1976) *Multivariate Statistical Methods*. New York: McGraw-Hill.

Nahapiet, P. and Ghoshal, S. (1998) 'Social capital, intellectual capital and the organizational advantage'. *Academy of Management Review* 32 (2): 242–57.

Nelson, R. (1981) 'Research on productivity growth and differences'. *Economic Literature* 19: 1029–64.

Nelson, R. (1991) 'Why do firms differ, and how does it matter?' *Strategic Management Journal* 12: 61–74.

Nelson, R. and Winter, S. (1982) *An Evolutionary Theory of Economic Change*. Cambridge, MA: Belknap Press.

Nonaka, I. (1994) 'A dynamic theory of organizational knowledge creation'. *Organization Science* 5 (1): 14–37.

Nord, W.R. and Tucker, S. (1987) *Implementing Routine and Radical Innovations.* Lexington, MA: Lexington Books.

Noteboom, N., Berger, H. and Noorderhaven, N. (1997) 'Effects of trust and governance on relational risk'. *Academy of Management Journal* 40 (2): 308–38.

Nunnally, J.C. (1978) *Psychometric Theory.* New York: McGraw-Hill.

O'Dell, C. and Jackson Grayson, C. (1998) *If Only We Knew What We Know.* New York: Free Press.

Ogawa, S. (1998) 'Does sticky information affect the locus of innovation? Evidence from the Japanese convenience-store industry'. *Research Policy* 26 (7, 8): 777–90.

Ohno, T. (1978) *Toyota Production System. Beyond Large-Scale Production.* Cambridge, MA: Productivity Press.

Ounjian, M.L. and Carne, E.B. (1987) 'A study of the factors which affect technology transfer in a multilocation multibusiness unit corporation'. *IEEE Transactions on Engineering Management* EM-34 (3): 194–201.

Pennings, J.M. and Harianto, F. (1992) 'The diffusion of technological innovation in the commercial banking industry'. *Strategic Management Journal* 13: 29–46.

Pennings, J.M. and Harianto, F. (1992a) 'Technological networking and innovation implementation'. *Organization Science* 3 (3): 356–83.

Pentland, B.T. and Rueter, H.H. (1994) 'Organizational routines as grammars of action'. *Administrative Science Quarterly* 39 (September): 484–510.

Perloff, R.M. (1993) *The Dynamics of Persuasion.* Hillsdale, NJ: Lawrence Erlbaum Associates.

Perry, D.K. (1996) *Theory and Research in Mass Communication: Contexts and Consequences.* Mahwah, NJ: Lawrence Erlbaum Associates.

Peteraf, M.A. (1993) 'The cornerstones of competitive advantage: a resource-based view'. *Strategic Management Journal* 14 (3): 179–91.

Petty, R. and Cacioppo, J. (1986) 'The elaboration likelihood model of persuasion'. *Advances in Experimental Social Psychology*, edited by L. Berkowitz. New York: Academic Press, p. 19.

Pfeffer, J. (1982). *Organizations and Organization Theory.* Boston: Pitman.

Pinto, J.K. and Mantel, S.J.J. (1990) 'The causes of project failure'. *IEEE Transactions on Engineering Management* EM-37 (4): 269–76.

Pisano, G.P. (1996) 'Learning-before-doing in the development of new process technology'. *Research Policy* 25 (7): 1097–119.

Polanyi, M. (1962) *Personal Knowledge: Towards a Post-Critical Philosophy.* Chicago: Chicago University Press.

Porter, M.E. (1980) *Competitive Strategy.* Cambridge: Free Press.

Porter, M.E. (1985) *Competitive Advantage: Creating and Sustaining Superior Performance.* New York: Free Press.

Porter, M.E. (1994) 'Toward a dynamic theory of strategy'. In *Fundamental Issues in Strategy: A Research Agenda*, edited by R.P. Rumelt, D.E. Schendel and D.J. Teece. Boston, MA: Harvard Business School, pp. 423–61.

Putnam, L., Phillips, N. and Chapman, P. (1996) 'Metaphors of communication and organization'. In *Handbook of Organizational Studies*, edited by S. Clegg, C. Hardy and W. Nord. London: Sage. pp. 375–408.

Randolph, W.A. and Posner, B.Z. (1988) 'What every manager needs to know about project management'. *Sloan Management Review* Summer: 65–73.

Reddy, N.M. and Zhao, L. (1990) 'International technology transfer: a review'. *Research Policy* 19 (4): 285–405.

Reed, R. and deFillippi, R.J. (1990) 'Causal ambiguity, barriers to imitation, and sustainable competitive advantage'. *Academy of Management Review* 15 (1): 88–102.

Rey, R.F. (ed.) (1984) *Engineering and Operations in the Bell System.* Murray Hill, NJ: AT&T Bell Laboratories.

Rice, R.E. and Rogers, E.M. (1980) 'Reinvention in the innovation process'. *Knowledge: Creation, Diffusion, Utilization* 1 (4): 499–514.

Rivkin, J.W. (2000) 'Imitation of complex strategies'. *Management Science* 46 (6): 824–44.

Rivkin, J.W. (2001) 'Reproducing knowledge: replication without imitation at moderate complexity'. *Organization Science* 12 (3): 274–93.

Rogers, E. (1983) *The Diffusion of Innovation.* New York: Free Press.

Rogers, E.M. (1994) *A History of Communication Study: A Biographical Approach.* New York: Free Press.

Rommetveit, R. (1974) *On Message Structure: A Framework for the Study of Language and Communication.* London and New York: John Wiley and Sons.

Ruggles, R. (1998) 'The state of the notion: knowledge management in practice'. *California Management Review* 40 (3): 80–9.

Rumelt, R. (1984) 'Toward a strategic theory of the firm'. In *Competitive Strategic Management,* edited by R. Lamb. Englewood Cliffs, NJ: Prentice-Hall, pp. 556–70.

Rumelt, R. (1987) 'Theory strategy and entrepreneurship'. In *The Competitive Challenge,* edited by D. Teece. Cambridge, MA: Ballinger, pp. 137–58.

Rumelt, R. (1991) 'How much does industry matter?' *Strategic Management Journal* 12: 167–85.

Rumelt, R., Schendel, D. and Teece, D.J. (1994) *Fundamental Issues in Strategy: A Research Agenda.* Boston, MA: Harvard Business School Press.

Rumelt, R.P. (1994) 'Inertia and transformation'. In *Resource-based and Evolutionary Theories of the Firm: Towards a Synthesis,* edited by C.A. Montgomery. Norwell, MA: Kluwer Academic Publishers, pp. 101–32.

Schein, E.H. (1985) *Organizational Culture and Leadership: A Dynamic View.* San Francisco: Jossey-Bass.

Schoemaker, P.J.H. (1990) 'Strategy, complexity, and economic rent'. *Management Science* 36 (10): 1178–92.

Serevin, W. and Tankerd, J. (1988) *Communication Theories: Origins, Methods, Uses.* New York: Longman.

Shannon, C.E. and Weaver, W. (1949) *The Mathematical Theory of Communication.* Chicago: University of Illinois Press.

Slater, R. (1993) *The New General Electric.* Homewood, IL: Richard D. Irwin Inc.

Slywotzky, A.J. and Morrison, D.J. (2000) *How Digital Is Your Business?* New York: Random House.

Stalk, G., Evans, P. and Shulman, L.E. (1992) 'Competing on capabilities: the new rules of corporate strategy'. *Harvard Business Review* March–April: 57–69.

Stalk, G.J. and Hout, T.M. (1990) *Competing Against Time: How Time-based Competition is Reshaping Global Markets.* New York: Free Press.

Sternthal, B., Phillips, L. and Dholokia, R. (1978) 'The persuasive effect of source credibility: a situational analysis'. *Public Opinion Quarterly* 42 (3): 285–314.

Stewart, D.K. and Love, W.A. (1968) 'A general canonical correlation index'. *Psychological Bulletin* 70: 160–3.

Stewart, T. (2000) 'Knowledge worth $1.25 billion'. *Fortune,* 27 November, P. 302.

Stohl, C. and Redding, W.C. (1987) 'Messages and message exchange process'. In *Handbook of Organizational Communication: An Interdisciplinary Perspective*, edited by F. Jablin, L. Putnam, K. Roberts and L. Porter. Beverly Hills, CA: Sage, pp. 451–502.

Szulanski, G. (1996) 'Exploring internal stickiness: impediments to the transfer of best practice within the firm'. *Strategic Management Journal* 17: 27–43.

Teece, D. (1977) 'Technology transfer by multinational corporations: the resource cost of transferring technological know-how'. *Economic Journal* 87: 242–61.

Teece, D. (1987) 'Capturing value from technological innovations: integration, strategic partnering, and licensing decisions'. In *Technology and Global Industry*, edited by B. Guile and H. Brools. Washington, DC: National Academic Press, pp. 65–95.

Teece, D.J. (1976) *The Multinational Corporation and the Resource Cost of International Technology Transfer*. Cambridge, MA: Ballinger Publishing Company.

Teece, D.J., Pisano, G. and Shuen, A. (1990) 'Firm capabilities, resources, and the concept of strategy'. NAPA Conference, 1990.

Teece, D.J., Pisano, G. and Shuen, A. (1997) 'Dynamic capabilities and strategic management'. *Strategic Management Journal* 18 (7): 509–33.

Terwiesch, C. and Bohn, R.E. (2001) 'Learning and process improvement during production ramp-up'. *International Journal of Production Economics* 70 (1): 1–19.

Tolbert, P.S. (1987) 'Institutional sources of organizational culture in major law firms'. In *Institutional Patterns and Organizations: Culture and Environment*, edited by L.G. Zucker. Cambridge, MA: Ballinger Publishing Company, pp. 101–13.

Tsai, W. and Ghoshal, S. (1998) 'Social capital and value creation: the role of intrafirm networks'. *Academy of Management Journal* 41 (4): 464–76.

Tyre, M. (1991) 'Managing the introduction of new process technology: international differences in a multi-plant network'. *Research Policy* 20: 57–76.

Tyre, M.J. and Hauptman, O. (1992) 'Effectiveness of organizational responses to technological change in the production process'. *Organization Science* 3 (3): 301–19.

Tyre, M.J. and Orlikowski, W.J. (1994) 'Windows of opportunity: temporal patterns of technological adaptation in organization'. *Organization Science* 5 (1): 98–118.

Ulrich, D. and Lake, D. (1990) *Organizational Capability*. New York: John Wiley and Sons.

Uyterhoeven, H. (1994) *Banc One – 1993*. Boston: Harvard Business School.

Van de Ven, A. (1992) 'Suggestion for studying strategy process: a research note'. *Strategic Management Journal* 13: 169–92.

von Hippel, E. (1988) *The Sources of Innovation*. New York: Oxford University Press.

von Hippel, E. (1994) '"Sticky information" and the locus of problem solving: implications for innovation'. *Management Science* 40 (4): 429–39.

von Hippel, E. and Tyre, M.J. (1995) 'How learning by doing is done: problem identification in novel process equipment'. *Research Policy* 24: 1–12.

Walton, R.E. (1975) 'The diffusion of new work structures: explaining why success didn't take'. *Organizational Dynamics* Winter: 3–21.

Weick, K. (1989) 'Theory construction as disciplined imagination'. *Academy of Management Review* 14 (4): 516–31.

Williamson, O.E. (1975) *Markets and Hierarchies: Analysis and Antitrust Implications*. New York: Free Press.

Williamson, O.E. (1985) *The Economic Institutions of Capitalism*. New York: Free Press.

Winter, S.G. (1987) 'Knowledge and competence as strategic assets'. In *The Competitive Challenge – Strategies for Industrial Innovation and Renewal*, edited by D. Teece. Cambridge, MA: Ballinger, pp. 159–84.

Winter, S.G. (1995) 'Four Rs of profitability: rents, resources, routines and replication'. In *Resource-based and Evolutionary Theories of the Firm: Towards a Synthesis*, edited by C.A. Montgomery. Norwell, MA: Kluwer Academic Publishers, pp. 147–78.

Winter, S.G. and Szulanski, G. (2001) 'Replication of organizational routines: conceptualizing the exploitation of knowledge assets'. In *The Strategic Management of Intellectual Capital and Organizational Knowledge: A Collection of Readings*, edited by N. Bontis and C.W. Choo. New York: Oxford University Press, pp. 207–21.

Yelle, L.E. (1979) 'The learning curve: historical review and comprehensive survey'. *Decision Sciences* 10: 302–28.

Yin, R.K. (1979) *Changing Urban Bureaucracies: How New Practices Become Routinized*. Lexington, MA: Lexington Books.

Zaheer, A., McEvily, B. and Perrone, V. (1998) 'Does trust matter? Exploring the effects of interorganizational and interpersonal trust on performance'. *Organization Science* 9 (2): 141–59.

Zaltman, G., Duncan, R. and Holbek, J. (1973) *Innovations and Organizations*. New York: John Wiley and Sons.

Zander, U. (1991) *Exploiting A Technological Edge – Voluntary and Involuntary Dissemination of Technology*. Stockholm: Stockholm School of Economics.

Zeigarnik, B. (1967) 'On finished and unfinished tasks'. In *A Source Book of Gestalt Psychology*, edited by W.D. Ellis. New York: Humanities Press, pp. 300–14.

Zeller, R.A. and Carmines, E.G. (1980) *Measurement in the Social Sciences: The Link Between Theory and Data*. Cambridge: Cambridge University Press.

Zucker, L.G. (1977) 'The role of institutionalization in cultural persistence'. *American Sociological Review* 42 (October): 726–43.

Index